2004 POE

ONCE UPON A RHYME

IMAGINATION FOR A NEW GENERATION

Southern England
Edited by Chris Hallam

 Young**Writers**

First published in Great Britain in 2004 by:
Young Writers
Remus House
Coltsfoot Drive
Peterborough
PE2 9JX
Telephone: 01733 890066
Website: www.youngwriters.co.uk

SB ISBN 1 84460 551 5

Foreword

Young Writers was established in 1991 and has been passionately devoted to the promotion of reading and writing in children and young adults ever since. The quest continues today. Young Writers remains as committed to engendering the fostering of burgeoning poetic and literary talent as ever.

This year's Young Writers competition has proven as vibrant and dynamic as ever and we are delighted to present a showcase of the best poetry from across the UK. Each poem has been carefully selected from a wealth of *Once Upon A Rhyme* entries before ultimately being published in this, our twelfth primary school poetry series.

Once again, we have been supremely impressed by the overall high quality of the entries we have received. The imagination, energy and creativity which has gone into each young writer's entry made choosing the best poems a challenging and often difficult but ultimately hugely rewarding task - the general high standard of the work submitted amply vindicating this opportunity to bring their poetry to a larger appreciative audience.

We sincerely hope you are pleased with our final selection and that you will enjoy *Once Upon A Rhyme Southern England* for many years to come.

Contents

Laura Winter (9)	21
Quincy Clare-King (10)	21
Liam Flint (11)	22
Hannah Fox (10)	22
Danièlle Collins (10)	23
Jack Kenton (10)	23
Jessica Keats (10)	24

Bramley CE Primary School, Bramley

Amy Stringer (9)	24
Katie Player (9)	24
Gemma Withers (10)	24
Neil Cockburn (9)	25
Francis Dredge-Hetherington (10)	25
Grace Harvey (10)	25
Jed James (10)	25
Philippa Treadgold (9)	26
Stephen Brownstone (10)	26
Rachel Francis (10)	26
Stephanie Alsop (9)	26
James Caldwell (10)	27
Jason Green (9)	27

Bricklehurst Manor School, Stonegate

Penny Richmond (10)	27
Emilie Thompson (10)	28
Louise Marshall (7)	28
Ana Sewell (10)	29
Isabel Harrison (8)	29
Emily Lawes (10)	30
Thea Williams (10)	30
Katie Aspinall (9)	31
Gabriel Wright (7)	31
Marianne Blaxland (9)	32
Evie Abbott-Wilcox (9)	32
Oliver Rainbow (8)	33
Hannah Message (8)	33
Constance O'Conor (9)	34
Louisa Thompson (8)	34
Alice Sampson (9)	35
Olivia Walsh (9)	35

Buxted CE Primary School, Uckfield

Cove Junior School, Farnborough

Christopher Maunders (8)	61
Leigh Dootson (7)	62
Robert Higgens (7)	62
Charlie Haffenden (8)	63
Henry Pickup (7)	63
Joe Levick (7)	64
Chenez Hardy (7)	64
Joe Sebastian Taylor (8)	65
George Gullon (8)	65
Leah Byrne (7)	66
Kayleigh Moffat (8)	66
Harry Richmond (8)	67
Tom Finck (8)	67
James Taylor (8)	68
Joshua Raine (7)	68
Nick Bird (8)	69
Jake Edwards (8)	69
Ashley Ryle (7)	70
Ryan Edwards (11)	70
William Davidson (7)	71
Jenny Strickland (11)	71
Samantha Still (10)	71
Scott Hewitt (8)	72
Jamie Ayres (11)	72
Chloe Gibbs (10)	72
Katie Gurr (11)	73
Kirsty Brown (11)	73
Leigha Roffe (11)	73
Alexander Haddon (10)	73
Humphrey Sitima (10)	74
Ben Rendle (11)	74
Philip Dooley (11)	74
Luke Bateman (11)	74

Craneswater Junior School, Southsea

Tom Warlow (8)	75
Imogen Rogers (9)	75
Philippa Kearney (9)	76
Emma Atkinson (8)	77
Francesca Ifill	78
Shanice Ali (9)	79

Jessica Davey (9)	80
Lucy Horsman (9)	81
Alex Magee (9)	82
Danni Silk (9)	83
Jenny Downie (9)	84
Cameron Clark (9)	85
Daisy Huskinson (9)	86
Georgia Kane (9)	87
Nick Vieweg (8)	88
Keturah Strang (8)	89
Hannah Mahoney (9)	90
Emily Fielding (8)	91
Dominic Laithwaite (9)	92

Denmead Junior School, Denmead

Victoria Melluish (9)	93
William Clay (9)	94
Rebecca Davage (10)	95
Robbie Boyd (9)	96
Robyn Davies (9)	97
Thomas Weaver (9)	98
Lauren Hall (9)	99
Daniel Agathangelou (10)	100
Paris Lockwood (9)	101
Lydia Galloway (10)	102
Graham Gissing (9)	103
Lewis Le-Clercq (10)	104
Hannah Sturman (9)	105
James Clowes (10)	106
Arthur Doble (10)	107
Jasmine Carney (10)	108
Ben Stray (9)	109
Michael Rees (10)	110
Sam Wardle (9)	111
Katie Talley (10)	112

Holly Lodge Primary School, Ash Vale

Rebecca Brennan (10)	113
George Green (10)	113
William Petley (10)	114
Lauren Sweetman (11)	114

Bridie Mason (11)	115
Laura Armstrong (10)	115
Georgina Pedley (10)	116
Katie Hunt (11)	116
Sarah Durbridge (10)	117
Alexander Taylor (10)	117
Charlotte Turner (9)	118
Gareth Downs (11)	118
Amy Bollons (10)	119
Emma Rance (9)	119
Sally Wood (10)	120
Megan Kenny (9)	120
Frederick Bragg (9)	120
Melissa Buxton (9)	121
John Rothwell (10)	121
Steven Turnidge (9)	121
Emma Morley (9)	122
Sara Daborn (10)	122
Lucy Dewdney (10)	123
Stephanie Sherry (10)	123
Jessica Townsend (10)	124
Rowanne Steed (10)	125
Hollie Louise Everist (9)	125
Shelby Parker (10)	126
Louis Manders (10)	126
Megan Allen (10)	127
Sophie Mansfield (9)	127
Emily Cato (10)	128
Abigail Lamberth (10)	128
Michelle Pendleton (11)	129
Nicole Trevena (10)	129
Tamara Williams (10)	130
Hannah Queux-Johnson (10)	131
Zakary McNamara (11)	132
Hanna Kelly (10)	132
Sarah Neill (10)	133
Charlotte McKeown (10)	133
James Merryweather (11)	134
Toby Scott (10)	134
William Batterbee (10)	135
Larna White (11)	135
Jade Woolfall (11)	136

Phoebe Leung (11)   136
Adam James Kenny (11)   137
Matthew Debenham (11)   137
Laurence Thomas (10)   137
Carl Sherry (11)   138
Josh Williams   138

Mayfield CE Primary School, Mayfield
Hannah Walter (11)   138
Matthew Sutton (10)   139
Guy Bryan (10)   139
Georgiana Hall (10)   139
Caspian Kingdon (11)   140
Jack Chapman (10)   140
Alice Lambert (10)   141
Paige Waterhouse (11)   141
Tommi Caldwell (11)   142
Joel Brummer (10)   143
Nicholas Kent (11)   144
Max Ward (10)   144
Francesca King (10)   145
Henry Noakes (10)   145
Joshua Rimmer (11)   146

Potley Hill Primary School, Yateley
Alexandra Weager (8)   147
Charlotte Dale (9)   148
Alexander Allen (9)   148
Ellie Conroy (9)   149
Laura Payne (9)   149
Lewis Trower (10)   150
Laura Hesketh (11)   150
Nathan Connolly (7)   151
Sana Haseeb (7)   151
Thomas Still (9)   152
Sophie Crisp (10)   152
Bethany Rosier (8)   153

St John's College Lower School, Southsea

Jenni Wilson (10)	153
Kristoffer Yeomans (11)	154
Jonathon Forer (11)	154
Clare Langhorn (11)	155
Emily-Jane Randall (11)	156
Louis Cook (10)	157
Sylvain Wear (7)	157

St John The Baptist CE (Controlled) Primary School, Southampton

Hannah Collis (8)	158
Megan Watts (8)	158
Abigail Puttock (11)	159
Jessamy Tucker (11)	160
April Palmer (7)	160
Daisy Chester (9)	161
Eleanor Shepherd (9)	161
Edward Gaffney (10)	162
Fay Sebborn (11)	163

St Mark's CE Primary School, Farnborough

Kimberley Martin (8)	164
Lauren Gray (7)	164
Dylan White (7)	165
Andrew Sanderson (9)	165
Max Dawber (8)	166
Connor Woodhams (7)	166
Joshua Smith (9)	167
Olivia Farrell (9)	167
Maisie Gowers (8)	168
Christopher Seargent (8)	169
Melina Mukherjee (8)	169
Rachel Harrison (9)	170
Tierney Martin (9)	170
Zoë Woodhams (9)	171
Adam Arden-Smith (8)	171
Jordan Wrigley (9)	172
Todd Cave (8)	172
Rebecca Howard (8)	173

Paul Feeney-Cooper (10)   191
Luke Warner (10)   192
Kellie-Marie Griffiths (10)   192

Skippers Hill Manor Preparatory School, Five Ashes
Jack Webb (10)   192
Jessica Thomson (11)   193
Holly Ellis (10)   193
Will Johnson (10)   193
James Barnes (11)   194
Louis Catliff (8)   194
Jessica Arnold, Naomi Brown (10) & Jenny Goodwin (11)   195
Natasha Howie (9)   195
Samantha Hedley (8)   196
Olivia Dorman (10)   197
James Wood (8)   197

Stone Cross Primary School, Stone Cross
Emma Christmas (9)   198
Will Mitchell (9)   198
Otis Jarvis (8)   199
Lucy Murphy (9)   199
Charlotte Reynard (8)   200
Vanessa Gatward (9)   200
Jacob Bradbrook (9)   201
Jessica Lees (9)   201
Sophie Holyoake (8)   202
Lara Standen (9)   202
Laura Jones (9)   202
Sofie Gown (9)   203
Jessica Graham (10)   203
Paul Stevens (9)   203
David Stevens (9)   204
Catherine Holloway (9)   204
Tarran Basham (9)   205
Lily Gatward (9)   205
Poppy Mallows (9)   206
Connor Rowan (9)   206

The Butts Primary School, Alton

Peter Bray (11)	206
Ana Chambers (10)	207
Louise Datchens (11)	207
Jon Bailey (9)	208
Emma Spooner (10)	209
Michael Barwick (9)	210
Shaun Barrett (7)	210
Katie Pearce (10)	211
Imogen Hoare (10)	212
Ellie Callow (10)	213
Ben Spoors (10)	214
Dominique Butler (10)	215
Millie Anderson (8)	216
Joshua Browne (9)	217
Sophie Ilsley (10)	218
Hugh Wallis (10)	219
Henri Best (8)	220
Cameron Lockie (7)	220
Owen Smith (10)	221
Nathan Lockie (10)	221
David Barrett (10)	222
Clarissa House (10)	223
Maddie Joint (11)	223

Velmead Junior School, Fleet

Kirstie Bough (9)	224
Jannat Ijaz (7)	224
Alexander Walton (10)	225
Claudia Rozier (8)	225
Jorgia Flaherty (9)	226
Sophie Astles (10)	226
Joshua Trafford (9)	227

Wallands CP School, Lewes

Zach Rowland (8)	227
Nathan Luetchford (7)	227
Lydia Powell (11)	228
Tim Herdal (8)	228
Rosie Barker (8)	229

The Poems

The Glass Window

The glass window colours trashed and smashed
By the bones of the old kings.

We watched the window being destroyed
Feeling angry, mad and sad.

Now the king's bones lie safe in their chests.
Now the window comes alive.

Patient hands picked up the pieces
And carefully put it back together.

And now through the wonderful, wondrous window
Bright light shines.
Now no violence where he lies.

Matthew James Shuttle (9)
All Saints CE Primary School, Winchester

Disneyland, Paris

I have a poem,
A poem for you,
There is Goofy and Mickey too,
But not just that, there's Pluto too,
So come and listen,
Listen to me,
If you do, you're as sweet as me,
So don't just go to bed,
Go to Disneyland, Paris instead.

Katie Benham (10)
All Saints CE Primary School, Winchester

Cars Breaking Down

Cars breaking down
Day and night
Rally racing
Slow racers, boy racers.

Buses, cars, lorries
Ready are the recovery trucks
Easily forgetting to fill up on petrol
Animals interfering in the engine
Kas, Fords, Vauxhalls, Citroens, Lambos
In case of emergencies police are ready
Nee nor nee nor the fire brigade go
Gutters flooding.

Down the river speedboats go
On the M3 on the way to Winchester
Winchester full of buses
Nights quiet, full of boy racers.

Andi North (10)
All Saints CE Primary School, Winchester

Candle Light

Winter night,
We bring out the candles,
Bright, flickering lights.

Movement around the room,
The shadows go by,
In the light of the moon.
The patterns are dancing,
Like shooting stars in the sky.

I feel warm,
Everyone is peaceful,
The calm before a storm,
Relaxing and beautiful.

Adam Silk (9)
All Saints CE Primary School, Winchester

The Girl Who Got Locked In A Cupboard

Abi, come out
You don't want to shout
You must not stay in
I will call your mum called Linne
Don't cry
Come out and eat a pie
Don't play with a pin
Or I will call your mum called Linne
Don't worry
No need to hurry.

I don't want to hurry
I found a curry
There is a rat
That is called Pat
I can't find the key
I will call Lee
Abi come out
I will shout
Everyone, go back to class
No one pass

I am coming out
No need to shout
I will bring the rat
That is called Pat
I have the key
So don't call Lee
I will not stay in
So don't call my mum called Linne
Abi, you're out
I will not shout.

Clöe Benham (9)
All Saints CE Primary School, Winchester

Shoes, Shoes, Shoes

Shoes, shoes, shoes
Everybody wears them
Ladies' shoes, men's shoes for lower prices
£1, £2, £3, £4, £5
Any price you want!

Shoes for you
Shoes for me
Shoes for everyone you see.

Shoes, shoes, shoes
Everybody wears them
Pigeons' shoes, pigeons' shoes
Pigeons, come and get your special shoes.

Shoes, shoes, shoes!
Shoes for you
Shoes for me
Shoes for everyone you see.

Shoes, shoes, shoes
Everybody wears them
Animals, humans, anything that moves
Come and get your shoes!

Fiona Finnigan (10)
All Saints CE Primary School, Winchester

Style Mumbler

Set trends, don't follow them!
So . . .
Find a shoe, find a shoe that fits you!
Make it fit even though you don't want it!
You just need to find a shoe that fits you!
I want one that's red!
I want one that's blue!
I want one that's black!
And I want one that's new!
Now I need a shoe, a shoe that only fits you!

Chloe Archer (10)
All Saints CE Primary School, Winchester

Journey To School

I'm going to school,
But I want to go to the swimming pool.
I've got to go to school,
And not to the swimming pool.
So I get out of bed and get dressed.

I'm going to school,
And not to the swimming pool.
I get into school, I am so mad.
I wish it was the end of school,
Then I would be so glad.

I'm going to school,
And not to the swimming pool.
I go into school and do my job,
I go in and I meet Bob.

I'm going to school,
And not to the swimming pool.
I help my teacher with the books,
And we happen to find a broken hook.

I'm going to school,
And not to the swimming pool.
She whacks my head with a book,
Thank God it wasn't the hook.
Yes, it's time for home!

Leanne Grace Garrett (9)
All Saints CE Primary School, Winchester

Daisy The Dolphin

Dolphins dance delightfully over the salty sea
Coming towards me, they all splash over me.

Its body sways from side to side, splash, splash.

Dolphins' disco, diving dance, dolphin dance.

Daisy dances delightfully, delightfully as can be.

Ceira Goodenough (9)
All Saints CE Primary School, Winchester

The Journey Through The Day

I wake up in the morning
And get ready for school.

I get to the school gates.
I see my lovely teacher.
She teaches me every day.

I say hello and smile.
The bell rings.
I stand very still.

I walk into my classroom
And start to learn.

It's lunchtime now.
I eat my lunch
And go back to class and learn again.

It's home time, wait for my mum to take me home.

I go out to play and have a laugh
And then go in for dinner and have a bath.

I get ready for bed
And watch TV.
I go to bed
And sleep all through the night.
Have a dream in my mind.

And wake up in the morning.

Zoe O'Connell (8)
All Saints CE Primary School, Winchester

Off To Mars

One day in my house,
I built a rocket,
And put it in my pocket,
Suddenly it started,
And me and the Earth parted,
Then I was in space,
And didn't leave a trace,
Then I was on the red planet,
And met an alien called Jannet,
She said, 'Do you want a drink?'
And she gave me one that was pink,
Then again my rocket started,
And me and the alien parted,
Then I was nearly back at my house,
And on the roof I saw a pesky little mouse!
Then I came down the chimney,
My rocket fell in the litter,
And I was home in time for dinner,
For dinner I had cheese and peas,
Then I watered the trees,
Then I went to bed,
And I said,
'Goodnight, Mum,
Goodnight, Dad.'
'How was your day, son?'
'Not bad.'

Andrew Eve (9)
All Saints CE Primary School, Winchester

The Ocean

I crossed the ocean, I did, I did.
Have you?
I saw a shark along the way, I did, I did.
So I got my lunch out and gave it to the shark.
It ate my lunch, it did, it did.
It went away then I said it must like mayonnaise sandwiches.
Just then I saw a dolphin, I did, I did.
It gobbled me up, it did, it did.
For a couple of hours I sat in a corner all bored, I was, I was.
But just then I saw a feather and I tickled it, I did, I did.
It sneezed me out, it did, it did.
The sand pulled me down, it did, it did.
'You're gonna die,' the sand said.
'Go away, I'm going across the sea, let me go!'
So I got my rope to pull myself out but it was no use.
So I got my gun and shot myself, I did, I did.
So I leapt to shore, I did, I did.
But when I got to shore I fainted, I did, I did.
And I ended up in hospital and I stayed there all night, I did, I did.
And that's my poem, it is, it is.

Ben Martin Woodward (9)
All Saints CE Primary School, Winchester

Friends

F riends are very nice to have,
R achel is very sweet,
 I like my friends, I like them very much,
E mma is my cousin, I like her very much,
N ever is horrible to me,
D an the pan man gives me and my friends pans,
S uzy from the sweet shop gives us free sweets.
    She is very nice to us.

Sophie O'Connell (9)
All Saints CE Primary School, Winchester

Journey To The Shops

It's the end of school, I am so glad
Because it's always making me mad
I jump over the gate and on to the road
To get to the shop and buy a load
I came out with a Mars bar and a Twix
And then I saw Miss Tweedlebix
She stared at me with her evil eyes
And then she said, *'Surprise, surprise!'*
She grabbed my hand and took me away
This was not a happy day
On the way there
She pulled my hair
Then she gave a tut
And said I need a haircut
I don't know why she said that
It's only down to my back
Then she came to my door
And knocked and knocked and knocked once more
Out came my mum
She looked really glum
'Oh my!' she screamed as she saw me
She pushed me inside and said, 'Thanks, Miss Tweedy!'
I knew my mum was mad
Because I was really bad.

Rachel Louise Crouch (9)
All Saints CE Primary School, Winchester

Smelly Things Like Horses!

H orses are smelly things, they eat, they drink beer,
O r you can say they smell like perfume
R oar, they say, na-na, they're not a lion or a dragon,
S troke their golden and silk fur,
E verybody loves horses.

Chelsea Kimber (9)
All Saints CE Primary School, Winchester

The Journey To Magic School

To Magic School one day I came
I found Harry Potter
And we played a game.
Our teacher's name was Professor Flitwick
One wave of his wand
And he's gone in a tick.

Now I am at home but dressed in my robe
All the other robes packed away
Ready for the use of another day.
I'm stuck with spells I can no longer cast
Because that was in my time
And that time was in the past.

Lana-Marie Sharp (9)
All Saints CE Primary School, Winchester

A New Puppy!

A new puppy makes me think of soft toys,
Soft toys make me think of old memories,
Old memories make me think of black and white photographs,
Black and white photographs make me think of my granny,
My granny makes me think of vegetable patches,
Vegetable patches make me think of vitamins,
Vitamins make me think of health,
Health makes me think of hair,
Hair makes me think of growth,
Growth makes me think of
A new puppy!

Zillah Cadle-Hartridge (9)
All Saints CE Primary School, Winchester

A Journey To Space

One night when I went to space,
I found it a lovely place.
I woke up in the middle of the night,
And I had a terrible fright.

I woke up and I was in the bin,
The aliens made a terrible din.
My ears blew off; I cried with dread,
I saw a man who had no head!

Don't be surprised,
If you open your eyes -
You'll see it's only
Your Uncle Fred!

Katie Cook (9)
All Saints CE Primary School, Winchester

The TV Bizz

I don't drink.
I don't eat.
I need electricity
To keep me with the beat.
I see everything
As you would.
I'm brilliant at making the right channel.
I can dance.
I can sing.
I can do almost anything.
But I can't show shows
If I'm not plugged *in!*

Abigail Byatt (9)
All Saints CE Primary School, Winchester

When I Went To Spain

We got on the aeroplane and swooped away
And landed the very next day.
We went to the swimming pool and had a dip
I found £500 then I got up and hurt my lip.
I tried to hide the money in the shed
But it was no use so I tried the bed.

Mum came in and stepped on a pin
Good job her slippers were on.
She found the money and said, 'We're rich!'
So we spent it in the shops,
Cinema and funfair.

After that we had £400 left
So we paid it to the bus driver.
When we went home we got ready for bed.
When we got up I couldn't find a cup.
Dad said, 'Here you go!'

So I had a drink and went downstairs
And granddad had a cat, we called her Holly.
We stroked her every day
Till we went home.
When we went, we paid £100
So we went on the aeroplane and flew away.

Chelsea Louise Wood (8)
All Saints CE Primary School, Winchester

Alien

A boy played for 5 years
Just sitting there playing with his cars.

2 years later just sitting.

After 3 more years his mum *had had enough!*
She said, 'Who wants to go to Alien Theme Park?'
'OK,' he said.

He went on the video games,
A *huge* statue of an alien
Was standing there.

He trembled approaching it,
He touched it
Aaah!
It stepped off its stand,
And said, 'Greetings Earthlings,
I come in peace!'
He fainted.

'Eeerh!'
He was at the hospital,
The alien was standing by his bed!
The alien's head came off!
To his surprise his dad appeared.
'April fool!'

Connor Back (9)
All Saints CE Primary School, Winchester

Space Poem

Space aliens are really green.
Some are hairy, some are mean.
One alien is fat.
The other alien has a cat.
It is stripy as stripy can be.

Their spaceship is black and white.
They mean no fright.
They have got a red cheek
And a black beak.
One has hair, one is a bear.

There are blue aliens, black aliens,
Two-headed aliens.
One like an oven but a different shape.
One Blake and one is a fake.

And suddenly they were singing.
One of them had a microphone.
One bad, one good, one Blake,
One fake, fake hair,
Wigs and pigs.

Like a monkey having a banana.
Peeling and peeling all day long.
All of them were singing a song.
All of them were tired.

They went to bed.
One had black hair,
Black nose,
One red, one does,
One Blake, one fake,
And they sang to the big, bright moon.

Simon Day (9)
All Saints CE Primary School, Winchester

I've Made A Machine

I've made a machine
That can twist, turn and run
And make a hot cross bun.

I've made a machine
That has legs
And hangs my washing with pegs.

I've made a machine
That has a head
And even fires lead.

I've made a machine
That took me to Australia
On the way, I got paler and paler.

I've made a machine
That goes faster and faster
Then . . . a *disaster!*

I've made a machine
That took me to Ayers Rock
I saw 3 boats coming in to dock.

I've made a machine
That has a clock
But it doesn't go tick-tock.

I've made a machine
That took me to Sydney
And then it climbed a chimney.

I've made a machine
That took me to a desert
Then there was a storm alert.

I've made a machine
That can lock up a chest
The rats are a pest.

Sam Stevens-Green (9)
All Saints CE Primary School, Winchester

Splash My Dolphin

Grey dolphin
Magic dolphin
Swim me away
Across the beach
Across the bay.

Grey dolphin
Magic dolphin
Swim me away
Splash, please dash.

Grey dolphin
Magic dolphin
Swim me away
To a far, far land
Where I can play.

Grey dolphin
Magic dolphin
Swim me away
Take me to that ship
Where I can watch the children wave.

Grey dolphin
Magic dolphin
Swim me away
Take me to the Atlantic
Where I can watch penguins slide.

Sophie Mears (9)
All Saints CE Primary School, Winchester

Football

F un on the pitch
O h, over the crossbar
O ut for a throw in
T ap it in
B rilliant goal
A ll you can hear is cheering
L eaping with rejoicing
L imping back to the changing room.

Stuart Gove (10)
All Saints CE Primary School, Winchester

Spheres All Around

My skin is all the colours of the rainbow,
My body shines like a light in the sky,
I lived in a pot; then I moved out,
I live everywhere and anywhere,
I have millions of brothers and sisters,
Most of them have died,
I die when I touch an object,
I like to fly high above the world below,
I move from place to place like a traveller,
I can see everything,
I don't make a noise,
Nobody controls my actions,
My skin is as smooth as a newborn baby,
My surface is an unusual colour, shiny and reflective,
I was born wet and unpredictable,
My parents didn't know much about me,
When I was strong they let me go,
Humans like to kill us,
My life ends suddenly.

(A bubble).

Georgina Teale (10)
Bonners CE Primary School, Uckfield

Jealousy

Jealousy walks like thunder on a dark night,
Jealousy eats like a hungry fox,
Jealousy is as green as a freshly cut lime waiting to be dropped
into a cocktail,
Jealousy tastes like mouldy vegetables in a compost heap,
Jealousy smells like a dirty kitchen after use of a chef,
Jealousy looks like a vicious guard dog hunting for intruders,
Jealousy sounds like a thundering volcano erupting,
Jealousy feels like a bad mood you can't shake off.

Oliver Rutherford Brown (11)
Bonners CE Primary School, Uckfield

Love

Love swirls on the beach in the sunset.
Love squeezes you tight through the night.
Love is like the colour red flowing everywhere.
Love tastes like crispy roasted potatoes with home-made gravy.
It smells like wild flowers in a grassy meadow with a slow breeze.
Love is like a mother holding her newborn baby.
It sounds like wedding bells ringing.
Love feels like fireworks exploding while lighting up the sky.

Kit Lyon (11)
Bonners CE Primary School, Uckfield

Bubble

My round body shimmers in the sunlight
As the wind blows me higher.
I spend all my time staring down at spots on the ground.
Sometimes when the wind blows me really hard,
My body goes from side to side, round and round.
For some reason humans hold me like a feather.
Children hold me quite hard but the wind blows me away.

Jay Marsh (10)
Bonners CE Primary School, Uckfield

Love

Love has millions of arms like an octopus.
Love is a loved one coming to comfort you.
Love is red like a hot water bottle recently heated.
Love tastes like a sweet cream cake with strawberries.
Love looks like a baby bird in flight for the first time.
Love smells like wild flowers in their natural habitat.
Love sounds like a bird singing in the morning.
Love feels like a hug from your favourite teddy bear.

Thomas Newman (10)
Bonners CE Primary School, Uckfield

Love

Love tiptoes quietly.
Love flows like a river from person to person.
Love tastes like hot chocolate on a cold day.
Love looks like a mother holding a newborn baby for the first time.
Love smells like wild flowers in a grassy meadow blowing in the wind.
Love sounds like romantic music on a golden sunset.
The colour of love is like a great big rainbow.
Love feels like a baby puppy cuddling into your arms.

Thomas Argent-Smith (11)
Bonners CE Primary School, Uckfield

Love

Love swirls on the beach in the sunset.
It wraps around tightly through the night like a warm blanket.
It is like the colour red, as red as spring roses.
It tastes like crispy roasted potatoes coated with homemade gravy
                                    on a Sunday night.
Love smells like freshly grown, wild flowers dancing in the field.
Love looks like a mother holding her baby for the first time.

Leighanne West (10)
Bonners CE Primary School, Uckfield

Bubble

I shimmer in the sun, high above the sky,
I live in a small pot with my friends,
Until I am pulled out and with a gust of wind I take to the air,
I soar through the air with many of my clones,
I'm as quiet as a mouse hiding from a cat,
And as harmless as thin air,
I'm as delicate as a snowflake,
My life is a short one,
After a while I disappear.

Thomas Fuller (10)
Bonners CE Primary School, Uckfield

Love

Love sings like a bird singing on a summer's morning.
Love walks down the street and cuddles everyone.
The colour is like the red sun making friends with Earth.
It tastes like crispy, roasted potatoes coated with gravy.
It smells like an exotic flower dancing in the wind.
It looks like a baby bird being rescued from danger.
Love sounds like a never-ending tune.
Love feels like your friend hugging you when you're down.

Ben Wells (11)
Bonners CE Primary School, Uckfield

Jealousy

Jealousy stomps around like a teenager.
Jealousy screams in your ear like a young baby.
It is as green as a lime.
It tastes like a school dinner on an unclean plate.
It smells like a swamp filled with mud and litter.
It looks like a stormy cloud swirling around slowly above your head.
It sounds like a thunderstorm smashing against the floor,
It feels like a huge wart on the end of an old witch's pointy nose.

Jake Rouse (10)
Bonners CE Primary School, Uckfield

Sparkling Ice

I'm as soft and delicate as icing on a wedding cake,
I look like shooting snowdrops in the fresh spring,
I come from high up, I don't feel the cold there,
I like showing off going side to side and round and round,
Like a roller coaster, thrusting and turning and looping,
I get treated gently and melt fast like chocolate in the sun,
I behave very cheekily because I drop suddenly,
I can see the whole universe up here, it's magical,
I'm as white as white lilies growing side to side,
Swaying in the fresh, cool air.

Simône Collins (10)
Bonners CE Primary School, Uckfield

Snowflake

I flutter from the sky like a butterfly on a cold, dusky morning,
I tap the ground and melt as if I am sweating in the desert heat,
I appear in all different sizes,
I'm shimmering icing on a wedding cake,
I live in the air and I change to come to you,
Saving you from the sun,
I lie there watching you walk everywhere.

Laura Winter (9)
Bonners CE Primary School, Uckfield

Fire Away!

I blast my victim with fire like an angry dragon,
My shiny body gleams and glimmers in the sunlight like pure gold,
I spit out my victims with a great thrust,
My long, white tail has three spikes that I dig into the wall like nails,
I have two massive jaws to swallow my victims whole!
And I can burn anything that comes near.
Beware!

(A toaster)

Quincy Clare-King (10)
Bonners CE Primary School, Uckfield

Balloon

I shimmer as I rise up to the silky sky,
I am treated with care as I am as light as a feather,
As I fly aimlessly over beautiful towns, cities and villages,
I see children being cared for,
I see people chatting away in the streets,
I get flung about as I tackle the rough storms,
As I am released, I get a tear of sadness,
As further and further,
I fly away through the sky.
My life ends suddenly,
Without warning,
And just as quickly as I was made,
I am gone.

Liam Flint (11)
Bonners CE Primary School, Uckfield

Happiness

Happiness walks down the street smiling and taking to everyone.
Happiness is like a tree waving its branches on a warm day
                                        in a cool breeze.
Happiness is light blue like a sky on a sunny day.
Happiness tastes like ice cream with different sauces
                                        in a crispy cone.
Happiness smells like lit candles surrounding hot, bubbly baths.
Happiness looks like cakes filled with melted chocolate that have
                                        just been cooked.
Happiness sounds like a bird cheeping in the early morning.
Happiness feels like a new baby's blanket that is soft and warm.

Hannah Fox (10)
Bonners CE Primary School, Uckfield

Rolling Rainbows

I am clear and shiny
My disco lights reflect the sun so brightly
I live in a tube of gunge until
I escape from the soapy prison like a convict
I float through the air and bump and swell
I drop and the wind dances with me
I roll like a roller coaster doing loop-the-loop
My life is short and exciting
I feel scared because all my friends are exploding around me
The children are jumping for me
I can see the trees blowing in the strong wind
And the rainbow shining over me
Making me sparkle with life
Then suddenly I explode.
I'm gone.

Danièlle Collins (10)
Bonners CE Primary School, Uckfield

Take A Guess!

I cover my body with tattoos,
I possess a shell that protects me,
My life is wedged tight together with my friends,
Sometimes I get packed away to an exotic place,
My manners are polite,
I give clear instructions to those who need it,
Humans treat me with care,
Everyone finds it hard to put me down,
I see all my friends being taken away,
Never judge me by my cover.

Jack Kenton (10)
Bonners CE Primary School, Uckfield

Jealousy

It sniggers at people pretending not to be jealous
But you can see it in their face,
Jealousy spits with disgust at people walking by.
It is the colour of freshly cut grass,
Like sour grapes, bitter and vile.
It smells like unwashed hair, greasy and drooping down.
Jealousy looks like a bull about to charge.
It sounds like a high-pitched scream ringing in your ears.
Jealousy feels like cold, lumpy, mashed potato.

Jessica Keats (10)
Bonners CE Primary School, Uckfield

Winter (Haiku)

Frozen cotton wool
Falling. Layering the ground.
Colder the days get.

Amy Stringer (9)
Bramley CE Primary School, Bramley

Summer Sun (Haiku)

Girls skipping about
In the burning hot sunshine
Soaking up the sun.

Katie Player (9)
Bramley CE Primary School, Bramley

Spring (Haiku)

Spring bounces to life
Making all the leaves crunchy
Lights up the morning.

Gemma Withers (10)
Bramley CE Primary School, Bramley

Spring Flowers (Haiku)

Flowers regrowing.
New daffodils coming back.
New colours appear.

Neil Cockburn (9)
Bramley CE Primary School, Bramley

Winter (Haiku)

Snow covers mountains
With hanging icicles like
Frozen spears breaking.

Francis Dredge-Hetherington (10)
Bramley CE Primary School, Bramley

Icy Crystals (Haiku)

Crystallised mountains.
Jagged ice dangling down.
The crystal drops fall.

Grace Harvey (10)
Bramley CE Primary School, Bramley

The Autumn War (Haiku)

Leaves parachuting
Bare brown trees rejecting them.
Trees expect autumn.

Jed James (10)
Bramley CE Primary School, Bramley

The First Snow Of Winter (Haiku)

Ready frozen ice
On a pond - frozen ripples.
The snow is now here.

Philippa Treadgold (9)
Bramley CE Primary School, Bramley

The Icy Grip Of Winter (Haiku)

The cooling sun turns
to ice. In winter's frosty
vice. Seas frozen clear.

Stephen Brownstone (10)
Bramley CE Primary School, Bramley

Icy Fingers (Haiku)

Icy fingers lay
Forming a crystal cover
In winter's blanket.

Rachel Francis (10)
Bramley CE Primary School, Bramley

A Winter's Day (Haiku)

A hard lump of ice
That can burn my aching hand
Disappearing now.

Stephanie Alsop (9)
Bramley CE Primary School, Bramley

The Winter War (Haiku)

Winter conquers all.
Icicles like frozen spears,
Smashing on impact.

James Caldwell (10)
Bramley CE Primary School, Bramley

Snow

Ice is very slippery glass.
Cars are sliding across the road, boom!
Burst tyre, slips and slides.

Jason Green (9)
Bramley CE Primary School, Bramley

Ghost Poem

In a dark and creepy prison cell,
where chains clank all day and night
and screams of imprisoned murderers
and thieves echo through the wall,
a ghost of an executed criminal
drifts and glides
around the cold and dark room,
silent and swift,
with a rope still round its neck,
with a frayed edge held loosely
in a gnarled, mouldy hand,
bulging, sticking-out eyes, staring
and popping out of a rotting,
translucent face,
an evil, scary frown
made the rotting face worse still,
in a dark and creepy prison cell.

Penny Richmond (10)
Bricklehurst Manor School, Stonegate

Amanda's Panda

Emily plays with her pet rabbit,
Amanda thinks it's a normal habit,
And it's not as special as Amanda's panda.

Lucy has a flash, new sports car,
Amanda doesn't really care,
She has a panda bear.

Eliza has a dolphin pool,
Amanda thinks it's rather cool,
But not as special as Amanda's panda.

Rosie plays with her dolls' house,
Amanda thinks it's more like a tree house,
And she has a panda bear.

Amanda has a panda,
All cuddly and neat,
And she thinks nothing's as sweet as a panda.

Emilie Thompson (10)
Bricklehurst Manor School, Stonegate

The Night

The night is a cool place,
a swish of wind, a shiver of a breeze.
The night is the howl of the wolf,
a slither of ice, a drip of water.
A curlew smoke with a whirling, twirling star,
the light of a moonbeam sliding to Earth.
A shooting star is a rocket drawing lines
on the black blanket of the sky.
The night is an echo of the eagle,
with deadly talons of the orange-eyed bird.

Louise Marshall (7)
Bricklehurst Manor School, Stonegate

My Family

My family is rather normal
And I think you will agree,
They're the most normal people I know.

My little sister can only just walk
But my big sister Saffron
Has just learned to drive.

My mum is always telling me what to do
But my dad is even worse
But I don't really care.

I have a big, shaggy dog
That never tells me what to do,
He just sits in his basket.

He learned how to walk years ago
But he doesn't really have a clue
But I love him all the same!

Ana Sewell (10)
Bricklehurst Manor School, Stonegate

The Night

The night is a velvet blanket,
Wrapped around a sleeping world.
The night is a howl of a wolf,
And the shimmering of blood.
The night is black cotton wool clinging in the corners,
And the cobwebs sparkle like dewdrops.
The night is endless and I am in my bed,
Tossing and turning, trying to get to sleep.
The night is a world of shooting stars,
A stream of light through the window onto my bed.
The night is the shrinking sun and the rising moon,
The day begins for the animals.

Isabel Harrison (8)
Bricklehurst Manor School, Stonegate

Me As A Baby

When I was a newborn baby
Everything was strange,
When I opened up my eyes
Boy, there was a change!

Everything was different
To where I was before,
I didn't know where I was
I really wasn't sure.

Above me there were faces
Small and fat and round,
There were funny things to touch
And lots of funny sounds.

Hands came out to touch me
But how I'd scream and shout,
They'd never, never touch me
They'd never get me out.

I know and you know
Of all the babies you could see,
None of them in the world
Are quite as cute as me.

Emily Lawes (10)
Bricklehurst Manor School, Stonegate

The Snowdrop

A shaded green stalk
Supports a delicate lantern
That glows white
In the fading light.
The three protective petals drape lovingly
Round the green-edged bell.
From the brown leafy ground
Come the smooth, dull leaves,
Followed closely by these miniature buds
That announce the coming of spring.

Thea Williams (10)
Bricklehurst Manor School, Stonegate

Dear Dad

Dear Dad,

I have sharpened my pencil.
There is a sum I can't work out.
What's the answer?
I've lost my pen.
Teacher is going to get angry.
Been watching TV for inspiration.

I've got to draw a picture
But I've lost my piece of paper.
Can't find another.
She'll be cross with me.

What shall I do?
Send a letter to teacher for me.
Please!

Katie Aspinall (9)
Bricklehurst Manor School, Stonegate

The Night

The night is a velvet blanket
wrapped around a sleeping world.
The night is lit up with stars
shining through the fingers of the trees.
The night is as dark as a witch's hat
or a cave where witches meet.
The night has a slight breeze
that knocks at my front door.
The night is full up with the smells of
my mum and dad having curry.
The night-time's friendly sounds
of my hamster in his exercise wheel.

Gabriel Wright (7)
Bricklehurst Manor School, Stonegate

Little Prayer

I am a little prayer,
I pray all night and day.
I never want to play,
Instead I want to pray.

I am a little prayer,
Praying is the best.
I am not like the rest,
Because I wear the holy crest.

I am a little prayer,
I pray every day.
And also in May,
I am very gay.

Marianne Blaxland (9)
Bricklehurst Manor School, Stonegate

Ice

When you drive on the ice,
It is slippery and not very nice.

You slip over and hurt yourself,
Your reflection is shown on the black melting ice.

Your car will not move on the black melting ice,
It is too slippery and not very nice.

When you walk on the black melting ice,
You're sure to slip over because it's black melting ice.

We try all day to walk on the ice,
But we can't because it's black melting ice.

Evie Abbott-Wilcox (9)
Bricklehurst Manor School, Stonegate

Springtime

Springtime is
Changing clothes
Ready
For the
Summer.

Hawaii is a place of sun
That always
Has the
Summer.

Hawaii blows the
Winter
Away and
Lets the springtime
Back in.

Hawaii has a kind
Of shelter
That spits
The
Rain away.

Oliver Rainbow (8)
Bricklehurst Manor School, Stonegate

The Teddy Bear

There was a bear at a fair
Who was sitting on a chair,
In the spring air,
Blowing in the wind,
Like a kite.

High above the clouds,
Like an aeroplane,
Flying so high,
Like a cat who can fly
On a trapeze at a circus.

Hannah Message (8)
Bricklehurst Manor School, Stonegate

Help Me, Lord

Children laugh at the colour of my skin
Why, my Lord?
I go to market. Somebody starts to serve me
But then a white person comes and they go away.
Why, my Lord?

People snigger and call me names to my face.
Why, my Lord?

I do not understand. People treat me like a plastic figure
That they can just throw away and be done with.
Why, my Lord?

I am black, they are white. What difference does it make?
Help me, Lord.

Constance O'Conor (9)
Bricklehurst Manor School, Stonegate

Mr Herbert

Mr Herbert is a sherbet,
Who burps every day,
Staring at the stars at night,
Chasing down the street.

Mr Herbert can't cook at all,
He makes the pasta fall,
Onto the dirty floor,
Where there's a big, black hole.

Mr Herbert can't teach,
He's too busy cleaning up the bleach,
Mr Herbert loves to play,
Even in the rain.

Louisa Thompson (8)
Bricklehurst Manor School, Stonegate

The Sad Poem

Sad is bad.
I'm so unhappy.
I'm always not glad
About anything with me.

I want some food
But nothing makes
Me happy.
I'm always thirsty
But I get nothing.

I see people get
Good food but
I don't.
I want to grow
Up as a normal person
But I'm not.

I go to the river.
I see the sad face
Of my reflection
In the river.

Alice Sampson (9)
Bricklehurst Manor School, Stonegate

Do I Have To Go To School?

Oh Mum, do I have to go to school?
Mrs Spring said school was off
And anyway I've got a cough.

Oh Mum, do I have to go to school?
I've lost my school bag
And anyway school's a drag.

Oh Mum, do I have to go to school?
It's mental arithmetic day
And I'd much rather go out and play.
So please, Mum, may I stay at home just for today?

Olivia Walsh (9)
Bricklehurst Manor School, Stonegate

An Unusual Family

My sister is a grunger,
I am a goth,
My dad is trying to be a pikey,
My mum is trying to be soft.

My family doesn't get on too well,
My sister and I fight and quarrel,
We're trying to get off to a new start,
Hopefully my parents won't split apart.

Today we're going on a family outing,
No more screaming, no more shouting,
No more slamming of the door,
No more stamping on the kitchen floor.

Finally, after that,
When we got back,
There was silence in the house,
All except a little mouse.

Natalie Collins (9)
Bricklehurst Manor School, Stonegate

My Auntie Jane

My Auntie Jane is simply the best
She is running all the time
Whenever it is time for lunch
She never stops to have a munch.

She runs all day
And runs all night
But never has a thing to say
When it's time to stop and play.

When she runs, I join in
But she runs around the whole town
It's the funniest, when I run round the house
And I want her to slow down!

Cecily Darby (9)
Bricklehurst Manor School, Stonegate

Who Is The Dragon?

There is a dragon
Strong as the night.
So I say
Good for him
Can he beat the earth below?
I don't know.

If you wait and see the horror
Of this scaly thing
You'll try to stay alive
Away from the green and blue monster.

You could be a scaly thing
Only if you try
Just like the eye of the monster
The monster with your mind.

In the spring
Of his mind
In his home
You will see . . .
Me.

Nicola Richmond (8)
Bricklehurst Manor School, Stonegate

I Am In Love

I thought you would like to know
I am in love with Penelope
I even asked her on a date.

I thought you would like to know
Penelope has accepted my date
And she's going to be my mate.

I thought you would like to know
I cannot wait until my date
With my mate Penelope.

Xaverie Wright (8)
Bricklehurst Manor School, Stonegate

I Want To Be Cared For

I wrap up tight, in my sack at night.
Out in the street, my small feet,
Cold in the wind.
In the winter I am so cold,
My fingers freeze and bread goes to mould.
I see people inside by the fire,
I hear sweet music coming from a lyre.
In the spring I watch the buds,
I see mums with their cubs.
I see the flower beds change their clothes,
I see flowers touch their toes as the wind blows.
In the summer it is very hot,
The red, pink and white roses grow in pots.
For me there is no need for the sack that I use in winter,
The tree's bark gives me splinters.
In the autumn I watch the leaves fall,
As though they're having a ball,
As they fall down to the ground,
In colours of green, yellow, red and brown.
I don't have a mother,
I don't have a brother.
I wish I had a dad,
I try never to be bad.
Please can somebody care for me?
Can't anybody see?
I want a mum and dad
To look after me.

Charlotte Wright (9)
Bricklehurst Manor School, Stonegate

Me At School

My brain doesn't work
It's really annoying.
I just cannot think
It's all a blink.

I'm falling asleep
Next we've got maths.
I hate school
I don't like it at all.

Maths is not fun,
English is hard,
I'm not very clever
I'll be like that forever.

I sit in class
With nothing to do.
I can't wait
Till I talk to my mate.

The teacher's talking
I'm not listening.
I'm so bored
I fake snores.

Nearly the end of school
We've got RE now.
The clock ticks past
I hope it goes fast.

The end of the day
Is the best time.
We can't wait to go
We don't go very slow.

Chloe Connor (9)
Bricklehurst Manor School, Stonegate

A Visitor

A visitor is a strange thing,
Who walks around and looks
At what you are made to sing,
And all your private books.

Then he has a small talk
With the rather embarrassed teacher,
All about beef and pork,
He sounds like a preacher.

Next he criticises our painting
To our annoyed headmaster.
He gives them all low ratings,
Oh, it's such a disaster!

After he left
We went to our solicitor,
And had a little chat
About the rude old visitor.

Fleur Nash (9)
Bricklehurst Manor School, Stonegate

My Brilliant Dad

My brilliant dad can run so fast!
He runs like a cheetah
And never comes last.
He's just like a blast of wind!

My brilliant dad is just like Jesus.
He helps me when I am upset.
He lets me go to my friends,
So I'm always having fun!

My brilliant dad's a sportsman.
He is a very good footballer
And great at rugby too.
I hope I'll soon be like him!

Olivia Mills (9)
Bricklehurst Manor School, Stonegate

Journeys Are Not All That Bad

Scorching back
Blistering feet
Scalding hands
Flaming legs.

The sun is killing us under its rays of torture
The sand slipping through our shrivelled, burnt toes
Flies hovering around our bloodshot eyes
Our camel is plodding along trying to keep up.

Suddenly

Shimmering colours
Trees or imagination?
Trees!
Salvation - an *oasis!*

The water trickling down my throat like a spring-fresh waterfall
The feel of the water on my body makes my want to dive
And roll about in the cool, refreshing water.
From sand and misery covering me
To water and happiness filling me!

Imogen Taylor (11)
Bricklehurst Manor School, Stonegate

Snow

When you drive past you see
Gleaming white diamonds on the grass.

People having snowball fights on the lawn
Snow biting people's ankles.

People crunching in the snow
With their woolly boots on.

The world has been sprinkled
With icing powder.

It looks like there is a blanket
On people's rooftops.

Lucy Close-Smith (9)
Bricklehurst Manor School, Stonegate

Let Us Stay

Look at the sun
Oh, come on, Mum!
Let us stay
For one day,
It's not long.

See the fish
And with a swish,
We could be following it
Through tall seaweed
And curvy shells.

Play in the sand
And on green land.
Look at the animals,
The elephants, tigers
And birds.

It's great! Let's stay
Or we could move
But we can't possibly go back
To rain.
Let's stay in the sun.

Catherine Alfille (9)
Bricklehurst Manor School, Stonegate

Letter From The Forest

The Amazon
Cave number 12
Brazil

Dear Mum,

I've got a boil on my nose,
My skin's turning blue.
I keep eating eyeballs,
What shall I do?

My nails are growing long,
My hair's turning yellow,
I've met a very handsome fellow.

He wears a hat,
He holds a staff,
He eats jelly babies
While having a bath.

Hope Dad's alright,
I'll send him a letter.
Give him my love,
Hope he gets better.

Phoebe Cournane (8)
Bricklehurst Manor School, Stonegate

Test And Then The Exam

Sitting down at your desk
Looking at your Geography test
No revision done at all
Knowing your marks would be awful.

Coming out with terrified horror
Hoping nobody would actually bother
Worrying about your test results
Thinking *well, it can't be my fault!*

No more worrying till tomorrow
Do you think that I could borrow
The answer book?
Just a quick, little look?

Today is the real thing
I really wish that I could bring
My teddy, he's called Cloud
But mum and dad says it's not allowed.

It's too late to escape now
Well, there's only one way how
Here comes Mr Oblic
Now it's my turn to faint and be sick.

The exam went well to start
Until it came to the compass part
I stared at the question, I could not think
All I could do was sit and blink.

The exam is now done
Let's go home and have some fun
I do not care about the test
After all, I am the best!

Rosie Gaston (9)
Bricklehurst Manor School, Stonegate

Moving On The Floor

There's something moving on the floor,
I think it found its way through the door,
That thought just makes me shiver,
I begin to tremble and to quiver.

The lights begin to flash,
I run and I dash,
I see green eyes staring at me,
Someone's glaring at me.

There's no one here,
The thing is near,
I feel fingertips on my face,
My heart begins to thump and race.

I feel a cold breath on my back,
Everything's gone, everything's black,
I open my eyes,
It's my *cat!*

Emma Thompson (11)
Bricklehurst Manor School, Stonegate

The City Noise

The city noise gives no peace,
Like frightened, honking, silly geese.

The city noise is loud and looming,
Ear-splitting, deafening and, of course, booming!

The city noise in the daytime is bad,
But don't let it make you sad.

The city noise is rather loud
Because there's always such a crowd.

The city noise at night, it howls
Like terrified, hooting owls!

But I like the country noise,
Not the hooting, honking noise!

Francesca Hastings (10)
Bricklehurst Manor School, Stonegate

The Candy World!

Could you imagine a world
Entirely made of sweets?
Most children could but adults would
Miss their 'healthy treats'.

The treetops would be made
Of fluffy candyfloss
And the grass would be laid
With sticky apple sauce.

My pillows would be created
Out of soft marshmallows,
Coloured in different types of yellows.

The large bricks on my house
Would be turned into large sugar lumps
And the smooth cement would be made out of custard,
Without those disgusting lumps.

So, could you live in a candyless world?
'Well, I certainly couldn't,' I'd defiantly whine,
But I do like our normal world,
In fact, I think it's just fine.

Stephanie Skarek (11)
Bricklehurst Manor School, Stonegate

Darkness

A cold breeze was blowing into the room
the coal-black night sky
seemed like a blanket
trying to smother me.
The air was still.
The stars were not visible
behind the dusty grey clouds.
The trees wavered,
but then stretched out
their hand-like branches over the fields.
The owl's hoot echoed
through the air.
The only lights I could see
were from the houses all around me,
but one by one
they were beginning to extinguish.
Darkness had fallen
and I was alone,
all alone in pitch-black.
But what really scared me now
was the wispy, white shape coming towards me . . .

Sophie Barker (10)
Bricklehurst Manor School, Stonegate

Let's Hear It For The Snail

Let's hear it for the snail
The thing that leaves a trail.

On its back it carries its home
But it doesn't have a telephone.

It has two antennae eyes
And it never cries.

It never sheds a tear
Even when danger's near.

The snail is very slow
Don't scare it or its head won't show.

Its enemy is a bird
But I think that's absurd.

Alexandra Alfille (11)
Bricklehurst Manor School, Stonegate

Let's Hear It For The Nit!

The thing that goes in hair
It lays eggs here and there.
It scurries in the scalp
It opens its small mouth
And gives you a tremendous bite.
During the day and during the night
Its legs are quite cool.
Its mouth is its only tool.
In a week or two the eggs will hatch
And you will begin to scratch and scratch.
But the thing I like best about the little creatures
Are its many irritating features!

Alex Barrington (10)
Bricklehurst Manor School, Stonegate

Let's Hear It For The Turtle

When the turtle skims water with its fins,
It thinks its flying with huge wings.
Its wrinkled head only pops out
When the coast is clear (I have no doubt)
From its green-patterned shell,
Which protects it well
Its beady eyes
Are smaller than flies.
Yet it's dangerously swish
At catching jellyfish!
In the sea, it's like an acrobat
On land, it's slow and fat.
It's easily caught and turned into food,
Poor turtle - that's no good!
Because no one could harm
A creature so calm.

Luke Boneham (11)
Bricklehurst Manor School, Stonegate

The Night

The night is a warm blanket of darkness
wrapped around the sleeping world.
The night is a cold time and only
the moon of fairy dust warming the air.
The night is a world of glittering stars
glinting on the crystal dew of diamonds.
The night is a great black bear
pierced through with stars of radiant beauty.
The night echoes the sound of sapphire streams,
bubbling lightly are the waves of the emerald sea.
The night haunts the graveyard
and echoes are heard down through the ages.

Hannah Gililand (7)
Bricklehurst Manor School, Stonegate

The Garage

Icy air
Cracked bottles
Smashed shutters.

The smell of whisky and lager
Howling owls outside
Spiders hanging from above.

Hunchback moon dimly glowing
Dawn is approaching
Slowly.

An old dolls' house
In the corner
With holes in the roof.

Rattling of chains
Creaky hinges
And floorboards.

The garage door is closing
Nowhere to run
I won't make it.

I'll die here in the garage
Farewell, my friends
And family.

Goodbye, goodbye, goodbye,
Goodbye, goodbye, goodbye.

Josie Duggan (10)
Bricklehurst Manor School, Stonegate

A Royal Fairy-Tale

Once upon a time there lived a queen
And for golden things she was very keen
She had her crown, jewellery and all
And she usually invited people to a palace ball.

They had sandwiches, crisps and lots of sweets
Not the sort of things you would expect a queen to eat!
But then one day they tried some new recipes
One was cheese, squashed bananas and peas!

'Yuck!' cried everyone when they tried it, 'yuck!
This is not a very good recipe, bad luck.
Oi, guards, guards, come here now,
We've got to get this new recipe out of town.'

The guards came rushing to a halt
And fell over like dominoes, *ker splot!*
'Ow, o, ea, ouch!' they all cried.
'Guards, you're all useless,' cried the queen,
'You're fired.'

And so it was, after all
It would be OK to have crisps at a ball!

Cass Michael (10)
Bricklehurst Manor School, Stonegate

How To Paint A Book

I started in the garden,
Waiting for the wind to blow
For the atmosphere,
Then drew the rough outline
To capture the fresh wind.
Then, as the pages flickered,
I gathered up my paints
And on it went into a shape.
I tried to stay inside the line,
Though this was hard work.
Next I got a tissue, but blew my nose first,
Then smudged it all together,
For the effect of course!

But, if the words jump out at you,
You're really doing well.
So carry it on steadily,
But not too fast.
The dictionary will chatter
And you'll definitely know
It's finished!

Charlotte Travers (10)
Buxted CE Primary School, Uckfield

To Paint Monkeys

First paint a body,
Then paint some trees for the background,
Paint some curvy lines for the tails,
Add a face or two for the monkeys,
You may need some grass on the bottom.
Paint the whistling of the trees,
The roaring of the air,
Maybe some rustling of the leaves.
Then hide behind a rock,
Without making any sounds.
You could add some echoing,
While the monkeys chuckle.
If the monkeys do not swing,
The picture will not paint itself.
As the monkeys would jump from tree to tree,
They would talk to each other.
If you don't add the arms to a monkey,
The monkey will not be a proper picture,
But if they stop chuckling, you will pluck a hair
From a monkey and stick it to your picture
To make it realistic.

Alex Ruiter (11)
Buxted CE Primary School, Uckfield

How To Paint Some Monkeys

First paint a cosy nest
With a roof made of leaves.
Then paint a hand of bananas,
A place to swing on for the monkeys.
Next paint some trees, some rope, some leaves.
Be very quiet and wait.
They will come
And when they do, be proud and watch
The monkeys carefully
And, if they jump and play their little games,
Then you have done well;
But if they don't play,
Then don't give up,
Just practise and practise,
Until the monkeys
Play and chatter.
Then, when one of the monkeys isn't looking,
Take his tail and write your signature.

Jordan Ball (10)
Buxted CE Primary School, Uckfield

How To Paint A Snake

First go to the swamp
Then wait for the air to turn cool and the sun to die down.
Let the sound of the bubbly, green swamp appear in your picture.
Make the smell of slime fill the picture.
Paint something old
Something rotten
Something mouldy
Something gloomy
For your snake to crawl and slither all over.
To make your picture better add the chill in the air.
Put all this in a murky, dark and quite kind of forest.
After that, wait.
Wait until the frogs jump
And the snake climbs on to your climbing object.
If this happens,
Your picture must be good.
When this happens,
You must slowly take the greenest snake scale
And dip one end in the swamp.
With the scale write your name in the corner.

Hayley Scanlon (10)
Buxted CE Primary School, Uckfield

How To Paint A Cat

First take a blank piece of paper
And wait for the right moment.
When you're ready, paint the whiskers
Blowing in the wind,
Then paint the eyes
And silky fur.
Next paint something simple,
Something useful,
Where the cat can relax,
Like a bed,
A soft, comfy bed.
If the painting's good
The cat will purr.
If not, the cat will turn away.

Anna Harris (11)
Buxted CE Primary School, Uckfield

How To Paint A Surfer

First I found a blank sheet of paper
Then I painted a blue wave crashing down
On a giant boulder.
I painted a surfboard,
Not big, but the right size
On which to fit a small surfer.
I painted the surfer,
Riding the waves
To the beautiful orange sunset.
I added a sunbed in the foreground,
Where a person was lying,
Watching the only surfer on the sea
And then I painted the last detail,
The people laughing and chatting.

George Cyster (10)
Buxted CE Primary School, Uckfield

How To Paint A Village

First of all, you find yourself
A blank piece of paper and a paintbrush,
Then a pot of water and a case of paints.
You start by painting a road,
Fading into the distance,
Not to the right of the piece of paper
Not to the left either
But straight down the middle.
Then for the houses -
First you draw them lined up against the road,
A little space for a garden or perhaps a tree, if you like.
Wait for a moment or maybe you'll even have to wait for a year!
But when you're ready, you might be able to draw
A little cottage up a dusty road;
Hidden by the small wood it is concealed in.
You will know when you have a decent picture because
The people of the houses will laugh and cry with joy!

Connor Macdonald Diplock (10)
Buxted CE Primary School, Uckfield

Down Behind The Dustbin

Down behind the dustbin
I met a dog called Paul.
'What are you doing?'
'I'm chasing a ball.'

Down behind the dustbin
I met a dog called Jake.
'Where are you going?'
'I'm seeing my mate.'

Down behind the dustbin
I met a dog called Matt.
'What is that you're wearing?'
'I'm wearing my hat.'

Luke Burrows (7)
Cove Junior School, Farnborough

Down Behind The Garden Gate

Down behind the garden gate
I met a slug called Jim.
'What are you doing?' I said.
'I'm singing a hymn.'

Down behind the garden gate
I met a cat called Jake.
'What is that?' I said.
'It's my Flake cake.'

Down behind the garden gate
I met a dog called Jerry.
'What are you doing?' I said.
'I'm looking for my berry.'

Down behind the garden gate
I met a lizard called Lizzy.
'What are you drinking?' I said.
'I'm drinking some fizzy.'

Daniel Dawson (8)
Cove Junior School, Farnborough

Down Behind The Dustbin

Down behind the dustbin
I met a girl called Claire.
'Where are you going?'
'I am going to the fair.'

Down behind the dustbin
I met a dog called Ben.
'What are you doing?'
'I'm counting up to ten.'

Down behind the dustbin
I met a boy called Sam.
'What is that smell?'
'It's my strawberry jam.'

Shivani Patel (7)
Cove Junior School, Farnborough

Down Behind The Dustbin

Down behind the dustbin
I met a dog called Fred.
'Leave me alone,' said Fred,
'I'm cutting some bread.'

Down behind the dustbin
I met a dog called Ted.
'Leave me alone,' said Ted,
'I'm trying to go to bed.'

Down behind the dustbin
I met a dog called Matt.
'Leave me alone,' he said,
'I'm flattening a cat.'

Down behind the dustbin
I met a dog called Joe.
'Leave me alone,' said Joe,
'I'm with my friend Foe.'

Emily Trodd (8)
Cove Junior School, Farnborough

Down Behind The Garden Gate

Down behind the garden gate
I met a cat called Jake.
'What are you doing here?'
'I'm trying to eat my cake.'

Down behind the garden gate
I met a squirrel called Mut.
'Leave me alone,' he said,
'Or I'll throw my nut.'

Down behind the garden gate
I met a dog called Pete.
'Where are you going to?'
'I'm riding to Fleet!'

Richard Hutchins (8)
Cove Junior School, Farnborough

Down Behind The Dustbin

Down behind the dustbin
I met a dog called Jake.
I said, 'Hello.'
'Go away, I'm diving in a lake.'

Down behind the dustbin
I met a dog called Ben.
'What are you doing?'
'I'm meeting a hen.'

Down behind the dustbin
I met a dog called Dan
'Go away,' he said,
'I'm driving a van.'

Down behind the dustbin
I met a dog called Jen.
'Move,' he said,
'I'm building some men.'

Down behind the dustbin
I met a dog called Dan.
'Huh,' he said,
'I'm kicking a can.'

Down behind the dustbin
I met a dog called Jake.
'Go,' he said,
'I'm only just awake.'

Down behind the dustbin
I met a dog called Pete.
'Move away,' he said,
'I'm gobbling a sweet.'

Down behind the dustbin
I met a dog called Lee.
'Go away,' he said,
'I'm talking to me.'

Jake Roylance (8)
Cove Junior School, Farnborough

Down Behind The Dustbin

Down behind the dustbin
I met a dog called Jake.
'What are you doing here?'
'I'm looking for some steak.'

Down behind the dustbin
I met a dog called Jake.
'What are you chewing?'
'I'm chewing a large snake.'

Down behind the dustbin
I met a dog called Jake.
'Why are you lying there?'
'I've got a bad backache.'

Thomas Bridges (8)
Cove Junior School, Farnborough

Down Behind The Dustbin

Down behind the dustbin
I met a dog called Ben.
'Where are you going?'
'I'm going to Big Ben.'

Down behind the dustbin
I met a dog called Tar.
'What are you doing?'
'I'm driving a car.'

Down behind the dustbin
I met a dog called Clare.
'Where are you going?'
'I'm going to the fair.'

Christopher Maunders (8)
Cove Junior School, Farnborough

Down Behind The Garden Gate

Down behind the garden gate
I met a cat called Jake.
'What are you doing here?'
'My owners are making a gorgeous cake.'
Down behind, down behind, down behind the garden gate.

Down behind the garden gate
I met a cat called Mate.
'What are you doing here?'
'I'm trying to find a lake.'
Down behind, down behind, down behind the garden gate.

Down behind the garden gate
I met a cat called Bate.
'What are you doing here?'
'I want a brown Flake.'
Down behind, down behind, down behind the garden gate.

Leigh Dootson (7)
Cove Junior School, Farnborough

Down Behind The Garden Gate

Down behind the garden gate
I met a dog called Fred.
'What are you doing here?'
'I'm just going to bed.'

Down behind the garden gate
I met a cow called Ted.
'What are you doing here?'
'I'm just lying here,' he said.

Down behind the garden gate
I met a cat called Lee.
'Why are you eating here?'
'I'm just eating my pea.'

Robert Higgens (7)
Cove Junior School, Farnborough

Down Behind The Greenhouse

Down behind the greenhouse
I met a dog called Dan.
'Leave me alone,' he said,
'I'm trying to get a tan.'

Down behind the greenhouse
I met a dog called Jack.
'What are you doing here?' I asked.
'I'm just scratching my back.'

Down behind the greenhouse
I met a dog called James
'What are you doing here?' I asked.
'I'm just playing some games.'

Charlie Haffenden (8)
Cove Junior School, Farnborough

Down Behind The Post Box

Down behind the post box
I met a dog called Pete.
'Are you very lost?' I asked.
'No, I'm looking for something to eat.'

Down behind the post box
I met a dog called Kayleigh.
'Are you upset?' I asked.
'No, I bark daily.'

Down behind the post box
I met a dog called Sue.
'What are you doing here?' I asked.
'I'm desperate for the loo.'

Henry Pickup (7)
Cove Junior School, Farnborough

Down Behind The Haunted House

Down behind the haunted house
I met a dog called Jack.
'Why are you sitting here?' I asked.
'What shall I do with my sack?'

Down behind the haunted house
I met a dog called Fred.
'Why are you walking here?' I asked.
'I was just going to bed.'

Down behind the haunted house
I met a dog called Tony.
'What are you doing here?' I asked.
'I am very, very lonely.'

Down behind the haunted house
I met a dog called Jake.
'What are you doing here?' I asked.
'I found a rattlesnake.'

Joe Levick (7)
Cove Junior School, Farnborough

Down Behind The Garden Gate

Down behind the garden gate
I met a dog called Tony.
'What are you doing here?' I asked.
'I am very lonely.'

Down behind the garden gate
I met a dog called Jake.
'Why are you here?' I asked
'I just ate a cake.'

Down behind the garden gate
I met a dog called Kane.
'Why are you here?' I asked.
'Because I was a pain.'

Chenez Hardy (7)
Cove Junior School, Farnborough

Down Behind The Haunted House

Down behind the haunted house
I met a dog called Speedy.
'Do you want something to eat,' I offered.
'No, I'm not that greedy!'

Down behind the haunted house
I met a dog called Eddy.
'Please can you help me?' he says,
'I'm looking for my teddy.'

Down behind the haunted house
I met a dog called Joe.
Why are you here?' I asked.
'I'm just about to go.'

Joe Sebastian Taylor (8)
Cove Junior School, Farnborough

Down Behind The Tombstone

Down behind the tombstone
I met a dog called Jake.
'What are you doing here?' I asked.
'I've caught a rattlesnake.'

Down behind the tombstone
I met a dog called Tin.
'What are you here for?' I asked.
'I'm looking for the gin.'

Down behind the tombstone
I met a dog called Kane.
'How did you get here?' I asked.
'I came by train.'

George Gullon (8)
Cove Junior School, Farnborough

Down Behind The Gravestone

Down behind the gravestone
I met a dog called Dan.
'Go away,' he growled,
'I'm looking for a can.'

Down behind the gravestone
I met a dog called Ted.
'Please go away,' he said,
'I'm resting, I've just been fed.'

Down behind the gravestone
I met a dog called Blare.
'What are you doing here?' I asked.
'I want my teddy bear.'

Leah Byrne (7)
Cove Junior School, Farnborough

Down Behind The Phone Box

Down behind the phone box
I met a dog called Claire.
'What are you doing here?' I whispered.
'I'm looking for my teddy bear.'

Down behind the phone box
I met a dog called Jim.
'Are you always so bold?' I shouted.
'No, I've just had a trim.'

Down behind the phone box
I met a dog called Ken.
'Are you always so lonely?' I said.
'No, I'm just waiting for my friend Ben.'

Kayleigh Moffat (8)
Cove Junior School, Farnborough

Down Behind The Wooden Door

Down behind the wooden door
I met a dog called Tim.
'Now what are you doing?' I shouted.
'I'm singing a beautiful hymn.'

Down behind the wooden door
I met a dog called Sam.
'What are you chewing now?' I asked.
'I'm chewing some old lamb.'

Down behind the wooden door
I met a dog called Ted.
'I'm still hungry!' he whispered.
'But you've just been fed.'

Harry Richmond (8)
Cove Junior School, Farnborough

Down Behind The Apple Tree

Down behind the apple tree
I met a dog called Claire.
'What are you doing today?' I asked.
'I'm going to see the mayor.'

Down behind the apple tree
I met a dog called Tony.
'Are you really a dog?' I asked.
'No, I'm just a phoney.'

Down behind the apple tree
I met a dog called Jack.
'Can I help you with anything?' I asked.
'Look for my old sack.'

Tom Finck (8)
Cove Junior School, Farnborough

Down Behind The Apple Tree

Down behind the apple tree
I met a dog called Josh.
'Leave me alone,' he said,
'I'm trying to look posh.'

Down behind the apple tree
I met a dog called Sue.
'What are you doing here?' I asked.
'I'm looking for the loo.'

Down behind the apple tree
I met a dog called James.
'What are you doing here?' I asked.
'I'm playing with some games.'

James Taylor (8)
Cove Junior School, Farnborough

Down Behind The Wooden Door

Down behind the wooden door
I met a dog called Sam.
'What are you doing here?' I asked.
'I've some leftover ham.'

Down behind the wooden door
I met a dog called Jake.
'Who are you looking for?' I asked.
'My friend Blake.'

Down behind the wooden door
I met a dog called Kim.
'What's up?' I asked.
'Ouch! My limb!'

Joshua Raine (7)
Cove Junior School, Farnborough

Down Behind The Post Box

Down behind the post box
I met a dog called James.
'What are you playing?' I asked.
'I'm playing a game.'

Down behind the post box
I met a dog called Ben.
'What are you making?' I asked.
'I'm making a den.'

Down behind the post box
I met a dog called Sue.
'What are you doing?' I asked.
'I'm just doing my hairdo.'

Down behind the post box
I met a dog called Lee.
'What are you chasing?' I asked.
'I'm chasing mad bees.'

Nick Bird (8)
Cove Junior School, Farnborough

Down Behind The Apple Tree

Down behind the apple tree
I met a dog called Jack.
'What are you lying on?' I asked.
'I'm lying on a sack.'

Down behind the apple tree
I met a dog called Fred.
'Where are you going?' I asked.
'I've just got out of bed.'

Down behind the apple tree
I met a dog called Pete.
'What are you doing?' I asked.
'I'm looking for some meat.'

Jake Edwards (8)
Cove Junior School, Farnborough

Down Behind The Dustbin

Down behind the dustbin
I met a dog called Coffee.
'What are you doing here?'
'I'm eating some toffee.'

Down behind the dustbin
I met a dog called Sam.
'What are you doing here?'
'My real name is Pam.'

Down behind the dustbin
I met a dog called Jake.
'What are you doing here?'
'I'm stuffing my face with some cake.'

Ashley Ryle (7)
Cove Junior School, Farnborough

Kennings Pig

Food-eater
Meal-beater
Mud-sleeper
Belly-keeper
Dirty-player
Heavy-weighter
Lazy-sitter
Smelly-litter
Tummy-filler
Insect-killer.

What am I?

Ryan Edwards (11)
Cove Junior School, Farnborough

Down Behind The Post Box

Down behind the post box
I met a dog called Ben.
'What are you doing here?' I whispered.
'I am hiding from some men.'

Down behind the post box
I met a dog called Dan.
'What are you doing here?' I said.
'I am looking for a can.'

William Davidson (7)
Cove Junior School, Farnborough

The Streets

Lots of people on the street,
Tall, small, making a beat.
Rubbish scattered everywhere,
Nobody takes any care.
Zooming cars racing around,
Money falling to the ground.
Colourful shops selling useful things,
Like stationery and golden rings.

Jenny Strickland (11)
Cove Junior School, Farnborough

Love

Love is bright red.
It tastes like hot soup.
Love is a huge rosy smile,
It sounds like calm music.
Love makes you feel special.

Samantha Still (10)
Cove Junior School, Farnborough

Down Behind The Dustbin

Down behind the dustbin
I met a dog called Jake.
'What are you doing here?'
'I'm eating a Flake.'

Down behind the dustbin
I met a dog called Joe.
'I'm looking for my coat,
To keep me warm in the snow.'

Scott Hewitt (8)
Cove Junior School, Farnborough

Fear

Fear is the colour black.
Tastes like sour pears.
It smells like dirt and grime.
It looks like a scary ghost.
It sounds like moving bushes.
Fear makes me scared.

Jamie Ayres (11)
Cove Junior School, Farnborough

Emptiness

What would it be like
With no one there but the air?
So lonely, so scared,
No plants, no living creatures.
Just emptiness would be there.

Chloe Gibbs (10)
Cove Junior School, Farnborough

To Be Free (Haiku)

Angels fly all day,
Gold is their special colour,
Fly away, be free.

Katie Gurr (11)
Cove Junior School, Farnborough

Dolls (Haiku)

My dolls come to life,
They speak to me like people,
I could play all day.

Kirsty Brown (11)
Cove Junior School, Farnborough

Predator (Haiku)

King of all lions,
A mane like a golden crown,
With deafening roar.

Leigha Roffe (11)
Cove Junior School, Farnborough

Heart (Haiku)

Pump, pump, its red blood
A complicated system.
Harder, harder, push.

Alexander Haddon (10)
Cove Junior School, Farnborough

The Grim Reaper

Someone with a plan,
A mission to kill for fun.
He is not afraid,
This monster works with evil.
Run! You are his next victim.

Humphrey Sitima (10)
Cove Junior School, Farnborough

Viking (Haiku)

Viking short, small, plump,
Sailing blissfully all round,
Axe ready to chop.

Ben Rendle (11)
Cove Junior School, Farnborough

Joy

Joy is red
It tastes like fizzy champagne
And smells like a rose bed in summer.
Joy looks like a red dragonfly.
It sounds like a heart beating.

Philip Dooley (11)
Cove Junior School, Farnborough

Fire (Haiku)

It burns everywhere,
Fire is turning up the heat,
A wild animal.

Luke Bateman (11)
Cove Junior School, Farnborough

My Street

In my street I saw
A wet, soggy tree
With rustling leaves.

In my street I heard
A colourful bird
Whistling a tweety tune.

In my street I touched
A cold, shiny lamp post
Shimmering in the sun.

In my street I smelt
The delicious cakes in the bakery
Being munched up.

In my street I tasted
The salty water quickly dripping
In my mouth.

Tom Warlow (8)
Craneswater Junior School, Southsea

In My Street

In my street I saw
A cat trying to catch a lark.

In my street I heard
The window-shattering wind whistling in the park.

In my street I touched
A silver, stunning lamp post
Lingering day and night.

In my street I tasted
Red and crispy bacon frying in the pan.

My street is just like happiness
Locked up in a can.

Imogen Rogers (9)
Craneswater Junior School, Southsea

My Street

In my street I saw
A butterfly with lots of
Pretty patterns like mazes.

In my street I heard
A yellow and black bee
Busily buzzing like an engine.

In my street I touched
A pretty little robin
With a red tummy that was
As red and rosy as
Santa's nose.

In my street I smelled
Fresh air bringing hope
And happiness.

In my street I tasted
The honey from the busy
Bees that live in my
Garden.

My street is
Really great. That's why
I live there.

Philippa Kearney (9)
Craneswater Junior School, Southsea

My Street

In my street I saw
A gorgeous golden retriever
Running like a zooming car
Going at the speed of light.

In my street I heard
A beautiful bird singing sweetly
Like a flute.

In my street I touched
A really dirty dustbin lid
With cobwebs and spiders
Like a haunted house,
Creepy and scary.

In my street I smelt
A fire burning quickly
Like barbecues in the summer.

In my street I tasted
The taste of chips
At McDonald's
And the burgers all juicy and round.

My street is
The most joyful, loving
And friendly place
In the world.

Emma Atkinson (8)
Craneswater Junior School, Southsea

My Street

In my street I saw
My next-door neighbour
Sweeping up the brown
Crispy, crunchy leaves.

In my street I heard
A cat screaming loudly
Like a car screeching
To a halt.

In my street I touched
The rust-red, old wall
And the bark on the tree.

In my street I smelt
The lovely smell of KFC drifting
Down the street and the fresh air.

In my street I tasted
My morning tea
As tasty as a chocolate bar.

My street is perfect
For me.

Francesca Ifill
Craneswater Junior School, Southsea

My Street

In my street I saw
A mouse munching on
Yellow cheese like a hungry
Lion eating its prey.

In my street I heard
A brown bird singing
Wonderfully like a flute.

In my street I touched
A pretty pink flower
As beautiful as a princess
With purple petals.

In my street I smelt
A piece of pie smelling
As delicious as a burger
In a bun.

In my street I tasted
Icy ice cream as cold
As a snowman.

My street is
A lovely musical
Kind street.

Shanice Ali (9)
Craneswater Junior School, Southsea

My Street

In my street I saw
A battered, broken TV
Sitting on the pavement like
Split black sacks of rubbish.

In my street I heard
The whistling wind blowing
Everyone over like skittles
In the bowling alley.

In my street I touched
The window sill all shiny
And dusty like an ancient
House.

In my street I smelt
The burning smoke rushing out
Of the window
Like an oven opening.

In my street I tasted
The taste of horrible dirt
In the bin, as dirty as
My brother.

My street is
A horrible, dirty place
With rubbish everywhere.

Jessica Davey (9)
Craneswater Junior School, Southsea

My Street

In my street I saw
Cars passing by the shop
As fast as racing cars
On the track.

In my street I heard
People coming out the pub
At night scaring me like
Mice frightened by a cat.

In my street I touched
A clean, metal lamp post
As bright as the sun.

In my street I smelt
The fresh breeze
Coming towards me like
A plane flying over my head.

In my street I tasted
The sweet and sour sweets
That taste like a piece of cake.

My street is
Fabulous, funny and fantastic
And I live in it.

Lucy Horsman (9)
Craneswater Junior School, Southsea

My Street

In my street I saw
Lots of winding weeds hugging
The pavement with greed.

In my street I heard
My cats screeching like a
Hungry hurricane.

In my street I touched
A purring cat as soft
As a chick.

In my street I smelt
The oven baking buns.

In my street I tasted
An ice cream with a
Great cone.

My street
It was the greatest thing
That ever happened to me.

Alex Magee (9)
Craneswater Junior School, Southsea

My Street

In my street I saw
A chip shop with chips
Crisping in the pan.

In my street I heard
Wind whistling in my ear
Like a bird singing.

In my street I touched
A big, brown brick
Wall, rough and sharp.

In my street I smelt
The fresh air all around me
Like cold ice.

In my street I tasted
The yummy, scrummy, crispy, golden
Tasty, mouth-watering chips.

My street is a kind,
Loving, caring street.
My street is a very nice street.

Danni Silk (9)
Craneswater Junior School, Southsea

My Street

In my street I saw
People coming home from school
Like elephants stomping through
The jungle.

In my street I heard
Loud cars zooming like a
Fast, spinning tornado.

In my street I touched
Along the red, rough
Bumpy wall that was
As tall as a giraffe.

In my street I smelt
Some freshly baked cakes that
The baker had just made
Which smelt lovely.

In my street I tasted
Some lovely warm sausage rolls
That I got from the
Big, blue bakery.

Jenny Downie (9)
Craneswater Junior School, Southsea

My Street

In my street I saw
Gentlemen coming home from work
Like a herd of elephants.

In my street I heard
Lots of screaming
Like a car on fire.

In my street I touched
A very rough wall
Rough as a calf's tongue.

In my street I smelt
Disgusting sewer pipes
Smelly as rotting.

In my street I tasted
The booming, lovely florist
Nice as Starburst.

My street is great
Because everything is fine
Apart from the sewers.

Cameron Clark (9)
Craneswater Junior School, Southsea

My Street

In my street I saw
A chocolate stripy, fat, grumpy
Old, moody, Cadbury's cat.

In my street I heard
The choir raising a
Wonderful Christmas spirit.

In my street I touched
A baby crying for
Its mum and dad
Like a whining cat.

In my street I smelt
The stench of the burning
And the frosty fiery
House.

In my street I tasted
The sloppy, slippery, slimy, snakey
Spaghetti.

My street is
A dusty, dirty place.

Daisy Huskinson (9)
Craneswater Junior School, Southsea

In My Street

In my street I saw
Green grass growing in
The cracks of the pavement.

In my street I heard
Leaves rustling in the
Dark, exotic tree.

In my street I touched
Some gorgeous, glamorous
Red roses.

In my street I smelt
Baker's sticky buns
All fat and round
Like the sun.

In my street I tasted
A crispy ice cream
As crispy as sweet lettuce.

My street is fabulous
And the best one you can have.

Georgia Kane (9)
Craneswater Junior School, Southsea

My Street

In my street I saw
A fancy, Ferrari
Zoom down the road.

In my street I heard
A BMW break down
Slowly and loudly.

In my street I touched
A slimy snake
That slithered down the sidewalk.

In my street I smelt
A chicken beautifully burning
On a barbecue.

In my street I tasted
A delicious lollipop.

My street is spotless
And clean in every way.

Nick Vieweg (8)
Craneswater Junior School, Southsea

My Street

In my street I saw
The bright yellow flower
Fluttering in the breeze.

In my street I heard
The whistling of the wind
As it flew past me.

In my street I touched
Crispy, crunchy leaves
As they touched my cold face.

In my street I smelt
The engine of the old
Rickety car.

In my street I tasted
The cold, bitter wind
As it hit my cold cheeks.

My street is
The safest place I could be.

Keturah Strang (8)
Craneswater Junior School, Southsea

My Street

In my street I saw
The sun struggle over the horizon
Warmly welcoming me to the day.

In my street I heard
The breeze as it silently
Stepped through the trees.

In my street I touched
A red autumn leaf
As it fell slowly to
The dewy ground.

In my street I smelt
The plants wafting from my
Next-door neighbour's garden.

In my street I tasted
The bitter wind as it
Hit my cheek.

My street is
Warm and welcoming
In every way.

Hannah Mahoney (9)
Craneswater Junior School, Southsea

My Street

In my street I saw
Two children eating sweets
Chewing sticky, pink gum
And spitting it out everywhere.

In my street I heard
The zooming of cars
Speeding down the free motorway
As fast as a rocket.

In my street I touched
A crispy, cold snowflake
As it hovered silently
To the rock-hard ground.

In my street I smelt
The scented smell of flowers
Swaying in the summer sun
Silently dropping petals.

In my street I tasted
The frozen yellow lolly
As I sucked it.

Emily Fielding (8)
Craneswater Junior School, Southsea

My Street

In my street I saw
A fast and furious car
And a Willy Wonker book.

In my street I heard
Laughter like a lion's roar
And people breaking Kangaroo Paw.

In my street I touched
A cream, crawling cat
And a big, black bat.

In my street I smelt
The big, brown church
With its incense.

In my street I tasted
My chocolate, smooth as silk.

My street is
Massive and very long
And sometimes very dirty.

Dominic Laithwaite (9)
Craneswater Junior School, Southsea

Misty

The night is scanning the day,
Wondering with mischief,
Snapping at the daylight
And tearing it apart.
The daylight struggles to get free
So it can shine again.

I hear a shock of thunder,
Lightning crashes down
Dissecting the earth,
Crushing my bones
And sucking in my breath.
I suffer in pain,
While the night chuckles
With deadly laughter.

Shocking shrieks -
I hear flapping terror wings
Begging me to come out.
Bats, like black leaves dropping from trees,
Glide and dance in the velvet-black sky.

The pale moon glows
Through the withering trees
And across the frosty ice.

Victoria Melluish (9)
Denmead Junior School, Denmead

The Rebirth Of The Gods

Through the noiseless but overcrowded temples,
Across the packed place of the temple god,
Around the swarming, waiting courtyard
And death crawls in the city.

We might Aztecs make
This awful, unbreakable
Sacred contract but
To renewal of the sun in the dawn depends on
The rebirth of the gods' power by human
Hearts.

A blistering sun blazes downwards
On the city of Cactus Rock.
The priests' festival of the
Ritual of the human heart.
The holy dance of the blood offering
To the waiting deities.

Tlaloc's snakes invade downwards
The daylight city burns with brightness
Tlaloc's muscular axe splits
A thunderbolt of life and death
A jaguar's roar bolts from his mouth
All Lord Tlaloc needs is honour.

My Aztec nation
Praises the gods
For our success and rain
So we glorify them.
The bitter thunderstorms
Hail down on the city of Tenochtitlan.

An unending, unbroken cycle of killing
And giving the gods their life
So they give us ours.

William Clay (9)
Denmead Junior School, Denmead

The Life Of The Aztecs

The people are content with their contract,
A savage promise.
They understand the Aztecs
Have to feed the gods
Otherwise our Aztec nation will not get rain.
Through the cramped but silent temple of the gods
Between the hushed but silent pyramid,
Across the hated steps
Through the silent courtyard,
Between the cramped skulls,
Along the Hall of Eagle Warriors,
Tlaloc's snakes slide down the dull sky.
A blaze of light
Comes falling.
A thunderbolt of life
Attacks the Earth.
The jaguar plunges from
His mouth,
The Aztec nation begs for rain.
The cold wind blows gently.
Around the sacred temples
The thunderbolt of terror
Smacked down on the ground.
The priest put on a dazzling white cloak
To show his holiness.
The silent crowd watches
In expectancy, fidgeting nervously.

Rebecca Davage (10)
Denmead Junior School, Denmead

The Aztecs

Between the packed buildings
Throughout the spooky pyramids
Along the cramped, packed Hall of Eagle Warriors
Terror walks the Aztec nation.

Beside the crowded temples
Along the side of the bloody, sacred skull racks
Down the steps of the pyramids
Around the sorrowful shrines
Horror swoops along the road.

Tlaloc's snakes thunder downwards
The sombre city lights up in fright
Tlaloc's body-ripping axe swoops across the dark sky
A crash of light, a death-revealing sight
Our Aztec nation has rain
We offer him food and gold
He gives us glory.

The people are happy with their contract
We will feed our gods with blood and hearts
Our Aztec nation is proud of their gods
We are delighted with our glory in war.

The sky was black
And Tlaloc's snakes struck again from the dark sky
The snakes lit up the sombre city in horror.

The priests put their pure white cloaks on
They took their obsidian knives
And struck the Aztecs' bodies in horror.

The Aztecs had a ritual
In the Hall of Eagle Warriors
They danced and reaped with laughter
And the sombre city lit up again.

Robbie Boyd (9)
Denmead Junior School, Denmead

A Night At Cactus Rock

Beside the blood-stained ancient stone
Inside the old Hall of Eagle Warriors
Across the anxious waiting crowd
Among the heart-beating drums
Death strikes the city.

Swirls of smoke veiled the evening sky
And smothered the dying sun
The clouds darkened and slid across the inky blueness.
Colours of pink, blue and purple as the sun set.

Drums beat as the people crowd
And fight to get to the front.
From above it is like a group of worms wriggling.
When the priests appear from inside the temples
There is a flood of silence as the priests rise.
As the priests kneel the drums beat faster
As the sun has its last peek above the temples before it sets.

Tlaloc's snakes fire downwards.
The starlit city blazes with light.
Tlaloc's sharp axe tears through the midnight sky.
A great thunderbolt of life arrows downwards.
A great jaguar's roar breaks out from its jaws.
Tlaloc needs sacrifice and strength.
Feathered serpents, people
Praise the deity
For life-giving power and rain
And honour him.

It's a contact, an unalterable tradition
An everlasting promise
An endless act to keep us alive
A limitless sacrifice
To give strength
For the rebirth of the gods.

Robyn Davies (9)
Denmead Junior School, Denmead

The Night At Cactus Rock

Among the frightening, crammed skull rock
Across the granite temples
And beside the silent statues
The blood-offering ceremony.

The crushed, noiseless
Hall of Eagle Warriors
Among the packed, blood-offering ceremony.

Tlaloc, the rain god
Opens his large, black mouth
The jaguar roars while his powerful axe
Flies through the stormy evening sky.

Snakes slither in the dirty ground
And awaken the dead.
The ice-cold rain smashes on the sacred temples.
Our unlimited promises of terrifying, blood-offering ceremonies
With blood falling from every corner of the dead man's skin.
The powerful god's unending promises of sunshine and rain
For food and drink and happiness.

Crowded temples with pleased Aztecs with happiness
For Tlaloc will repay us.

Our black-dressed priests sacrificing our people
For the gods.
Our terrifying ceremonies
Filled with blood dripping.

Thomas Weaver (9)
Denmead Junior School, Denmead

Aztec Temples

Across the silent courtyard
Along the echoing streets
Around the calm, smooth Lake Texcoco
Love spreads and fills our hearts.

Tlaloc raised his snakes of yellow light
He struck and the city flashes
Tlaloc's powerful axe ripped across the sky
With a mighty roar.

The morning light glows on the land
A storm begins to brew
Then the rain comes hammering down.

The priests led the child up the steps
We hold his arms and legs
Then I hear the stab of the knife
And blood comes gushing down.
We stand back and the priests hold up the heart.

The crowd was looking up
The family of the boy was crying
And so were friends.

Our everlasting contract
Our endless promise binding
Our eternal and binding undertaking to Tlaloc
For the rain to grow our plants.

Lauren Hall (9)
Denmead Junior School, Denmead

The Rebirth Of The Gods

Across the silent but crowded temples
Around the murderous pyramids
And among the smoking palaces
Sorrow fills the air
Across the sacred precincts of gold
Around the dreaded Hall of the Eagle Warriors.

The stone-cold weather swarmed the crowd,
Our priests come and praise
The body was ashes, ashes
Our priests come and summon the spirits of the
Dead, dead, dead
The dead awaken from the skull racks
Our priests revive the gods.

Tlaloc, the rain god, pierces the night
With his blasting blaze of light
He pleads for blood to revive himself
And hearts to bring him rebirth
The humans worship him, praise him even
For his powerful, almighty powers.

We Aztecs are immovable from this revolting promise
To feed the dreaded god Tlaloc
He pleads for our blood
And our hearts
To bring him to life once again
We must swear to never break
This forbidden promise.

Daniel Agathangelou (10)
Denmead Junior School, Denmead

An Evening in Tenochitlan

Beside the overcrowded temple,
Along the noiseless, hushed streets,
Through the waiting courtyard,
Across the silent, hushed Place of the Temple Gods,
Around the waiting Lake Texcoco,
Among the swarming, sacred, festival procession,
Hope spreads and fills our hearts.

The evening light is blistering on the horizon,
Clouds start to form in the sky,
Rain bushes down, down and down.

Tlaloc's deep mouth opens,
The jaguar roars,
His axe swoops across the sky,
A thunderbolt explodes in the dry evening air.

Our everlasting promise,
Our irrevocable contract,
Our eternal and binding undertaking
To Tlaloc for the rain to grow our maize.

There are millions of people lined in rows,
The crowds are silent and praying.

The priests emerge from the dismal cave,
A priest raised a bowl of red blood,
The rest of the priests started to wave their arms around and dance.

Paris Lockwood (9)
Denmead Junior School, Denmead

My Life

I stand on top of the silent but packed temple.
I look around, looking at the glistening
Countryside in my hands.
A sad but powerful life beyond me.
I see the happy life of children in my thumping head.
Not anymore, everyone's lives are ending.
I see crowds of holy people cheering for my death.
A sacred ceremony for me, my people show me affection.

Between the silent but packed temples,
Through the crammed pyramids,
Around the full skull racks,
Death strikes the city.

We feed the gods with glory.
A hateful sight.
Our everlasting promise to the mighty powerful gods.
Our timeless, unbreakable contract to the gods.

The blaze of the rising sun
Strikes the pained city in horror.
We praise the holy sky in a sacred ceremony,
The place of flowers is crowded with people.
A silent city of crowds waiting, waiting.
The prayers of our people rise into the cool, morning air,
Making it stronger.
Our promises to the hopeful gods is stronger
More powerful than our short lives . . .

The sky turns blood-red, fiery-orange and yellow.
The smoke of the torches fills the sky with thick, black smoke.
The time has come for the priests.
The crowd is frightened.
The temple steps call for the priests.

The holy priests slowly walk from behind the sacred temples
Up the steep steps and through the painted doors.

I hold our blade in a holy spirit.
The threat from the child's tear is given to the holy god Tlaloc.
The blood-offering sacrifice is strong and powerful.

Lydia Galloway (10)
Denmead Junior School, Denmead

A Night At Tenochtitlan

The stone-cold weather swarmed the crowds for miles and miles.
Along the sullen, granite skull racks,
Among swarmers of the festive sacrifice,
Throughout the hushed grounds of the Hall of the Eagle Warriors,
Across bloodthirsty plains in swarms and swarms.

Our priests come and kneel, kneel, kneel.
The body was burnt, burnt, burnt.
Our priests come and summon the spirits of the dead, dead, dead.
The dead awake from the granite skull racks, racks, racks.
Our priests rebirth the gods, gods, gods.

Smoking Mirror ponders.
Who will be rich?
Who will be poor?
The lucky, the unlucky?
He gazes into his ancient obsidian mirror.
Seeing our Aztec nation beseeching the deities.
He morphs into Smoking Mirror's shadow
Then feeling stronger, stronger, stronger.

The child's heart was given to Tlaloc, Tlaloc, Tlaloc
Giving the gods the gory meal of life.
Shattering the people's delicate lives for the hearts, for the food.
Then Smoking Mirror felt stronger as the men died.
The treaty was signed, the eternal treaty was signed
The food was signed.
The eternal life was given to the nation, the Aztec nation.
The treaty was signed, the sacrifice was taken.

The crowds come and pray, pray, pray to the deity.

Graham Gissing (9)
Denmead Junior School, Denmead

Aztec Sacrifice

Tlaloc, the rain god, sends
A mighty storm onto Cactus Rock.
His thunder axe
Shooting out blasts of thunder.
He controls the sky
Making storms and rain.
He controls light.

Tlaloc flies swiftly around the city
Sending his mighty powers
Around the island city.
His jaguar roar rings for miles
Defeating the people of Cactus Rock.

The Aztec nation promise to keep the gods pleased.
They feed them for infinity
Offering human hearts.
The gods promise to give a gift of rain and sun.
The Aztec nation grow their crops.

Between the streets people were scattered.
Along the roads people were cramped.
Among the pyramids people looked like ants.
Death ran around the streets.

Beside the Hall of the Eagle Warriors
The hall was packed.
Around the Place of Herons
Lake Texcoco shone.
Across the place of mosquitoes
The priests were busy eating in their quiet temples.

Lewis Le-Clercq (10)
Denmead Junior School, Denmead

Quetzalcóatl

Through the silent, hushed streets
Across the swarming courtyard
Around the waiting skull rack
Happiness walks through the courtyard.

Throughout the noiseless, hushed temples
Along the cramped city streets
Between the waiting skull rack
Death stalks the city streets.

Our Aztec nation summons Quetzalcóatl
Dawn creeps across the sky
The feathered serpent has long, red feathers
All around his body
And he wiggles out of his cave
That's dark and dusty.

The stars are shining in the night sky
The weather is cold like ice
The rain is like thunderbolts shooting from the sky
The weather is thundering with snow.

Hummingbird god quivers
His beautiful feathers glowing
Watching blood flow down from the temples.
The people gasp in shock and horror
Thinking they will be next.
Spots of blood dripped own the temple steps
Everywhere - dropping
    Dripping
        Falling
            Splashing

The priests are sharpening their knives
They are getting ready to kill some people
The priests look very happy.

Hannah Sturman (9)
Denmead Junior School, Denmead

Aztec Sacrifice

Above the noiseless, hushed Hall of the Eagle Warriors
Around the halted skull rack
Over the crowded Lake Texcoco
Evil swarms skull rock.

People watch in fear
As men, women and children are sacrificed.
The priest cuts them open
And pulls out the heart.

Through the hesitating, lingering pyramids
Along the jostling streets
Amongst the hushed temples
Death stalks.

Our Aztec nation summons Quetzalcóatl
Dawn wriggles across the sky
The feathered serpent has long, green feathers
All around his body
And he wriggles out of his damp cave.

The sun is rising in the sea-blue sky
The wind is nowhere to be felt in the air.

Hummingbird god quivers
His beautiful feathers glowing
Watching blood flow down the temples.
The people gasp in shock and horror
Thinking they will be next.
Spots of blood drip down the temple steps
Everywhere - dropping
     Dripping
          Falling
               Splashing.
Splashing through shocked streets.

James Clowes (10)
Denmead Junior School, Denmead

Aztec Sacrifice

Our unalterable contract with the gods
Keeps us alive
We give blood and hearts to the gods
And in return we get life
We watch in horror as slaves and enemy heroes
Are sacrificed.

Tlaloc's snakes streak Earthwards
The midnight sky is filled with light
Tlaloc's overwhelming axe
Tears across the sky
A thunderbolt of doom
Tlaloc needs blood to live.

We plead for life-giving rain
Tlaloc's jaguar roars of thunder
Around the hesitating temples
Beside the silent Hall of the Eagle Warriors
Across the cramped, dusty streets
Death stalks the city.

A blistering sun burns down
Upon the city of Tenchiltlan
The air is humid
And the Lake Texcoco is on the verge of evaporation.

The priests dance their sacred dance
They writhe and sway
Like the wind.

The knife is brought down
The ribs are torn apart
The heart is drawn out
It is shown to the crowd
Then raised up to the god Tlaloc.

The lifeless child
Is kicked down the steps.

Arthur Doble (10)
Denmead Junior School, Denmead

The Sacrifice

Beside the silent, cramped people, I stay out of view
Looking up at the hopeless prisoner
Not knowing what to do.
The stone of death waits on top of the powerful temple.
The tall temples around me cast shadows of the spirits of the dead.
Hunting the long, dusty roads for revenge.
The roads run down long alleyways
The sounds of the city are trapped in the walls' grasp.
The houses and shops are dark with fear.

Tlaloc hurls the snakes with great anger
Lighting up the midnight sky as they travel.
Tlaloc's mighty roar erupts from his mouth
Filling the sky with a deafening sound.
He raises his powerful, painful axe
And sends another roar of anger.
The thunder of life and death.
The Aztec people beg for rain
To help crops grow.
Tlaloc needs praise, or Aztec nation beseeches the deity
Praying for life-giving rain.

Our everlasting contract
We feed them our hearts and our own blood
And they keep us safe and help us triumph over others.
It works.
We give them things and in return they give us victory and glory.
It's getting colder and colder
The sky is rumbling
With thunder and lightning
Filling the air with another call of anger.

The crowds stand waiting
Waiting;
I can hear the cries of the prisoner
Not knowing which way to turn.
The cry of agony fills the air.
Everyone gasps.
The blazing fire spits out hot sparks.
The alarming dagger rises.

The cries fill the atmosphere
Sending a chill down my spine.
I stand there watching
Waiting for it all to begin again.

Jasmine Carney (10)
Denmead Junior School, Denmead

Sea Poem

The sea is a demon
Destructively slashing against the granite boulders.
She sends the angry breakers to drown
The craggy outcrops.

The sea is an artist
Carving the rough boulders
Into smooth outcrops of rock.
She wears away the rough outcrops
To turn them into dark caves.

The sea is chameleon-like
Always changing her mind.
One minute it's as rough as a lion
The next it's as calm as the dark, night sky.

The sea is a chaos-creator
Rumbling around to form whirlpools.
Sucking everything around it.
Nothing can escape the mad-minded waves!

Ben Stray (9)
Denmead Junior School, Denmead

Death Descends Over Cactus Rock

Beside the sacred temple
Among the waiting passer-by
Throughout the hushed palaces
Death roams the city.
Over the sombre loneliness
Around the burning braziers
Beside the ancient courtyards
Death descends over Cactus Rock.

We offer the gods eternal life in return for protection
The everlasting contract concealed in sheer violence
Shrieks and screams fill the air
The ceremony disgusts all our people
But it is in favour of all our gods
And we know that some day
Quetzalcóatl will return
To his loyal people.

The suspense rises
The priests begin their holy dance
Swirling their arms in the air.
They have the responsibility
Of human sacrifice.

The tension mounts
The blood drips slowly, trickling down the holy pyramid.
Death smothers Cactus Rock.
The priests perform their sacred dance
In the red blood aura.
The sun blazes down
Suffocating Cactus Rock.

The astonished crowd surround the steps
Staring at the sacrificed hero.
A cold shiver runs up their spines.

The clouds grow darker
They swiftly scud across the sky.
Uncertainty floods our people's minds.
A storm begins to brew.

Tlaloc's mighty axe assassinates the midnight sky.
His serpents strike downwards
And the midnight city illuminates like fire.
A jaguar's growling roar erupts from his mouth.
A blot of life.

Tlaloc demands human hearts
In return for natural life.
The people of Quetzalcóatl tremble
Honouring the deity
And praising and pleading for the life-giving rain.

Michael Rees (10)
Denmead Junior School, Denmead

The Horrific Bats Fly Tonight

The impenetrable, blind night stifles
The daylight
Smothering the last burst of strength
From the diminished sun.
A sombre blackness
Suffocating the feeble sun.

The tree wails as
The tempestuous gusts
Thrash wildly against the crooked
Branches of the ancient redwood.

The aloof moon
Stares down on the Earth
Like a vast eye in the
Overcast sky.

The horrific bats
Fly tonight.

Sam Wardle (9)
Denmead Junior School, Denmead

A Night In Cactus Rock!

The night sky still
Like an ink-blue sheet hanging in the air.
Dotted all over with bright stars
Twinkling in the moonlight.

Drums beating
The priests rise from their darkened temples
And the crowds remain silent.

Tlaloc's snake hurls downwards
With the roar of a jaguar.
With a single flash
The night sky is ablaze.
A jaguar roars once again.

He needs glory.
Our Aztec nation praises the deity
For life-giving rain
And we honour the gods.

Beside the silent, hushed steps
Through the crowded precinct
Among the jostling palaces
The procession draws near.

The knife pierces the child's chest.
A scream of anger.
Tears drip slowly down from her face.
Blood dripping from the stone.
Horror . . .
    Horror . . .
        Horror . . .

It's holy, we feed them and they keep us alive
An everlasting contact
A promise that lasts forever
Our promise to feed the deities.

Katie Talley (10)
Denmead Junior School, Denmead

Playground

Children in the playground
Running round and round
Some eating fruit
One looking at the ground.
Everyone playing happily
Some playing 'It'
And some just sit.
But one little girl sitting all alone
She looks up and kicks a stone
Across the ground.
Then the whistle is blown
And everyone runs to line up
And the little girl is left all alone.

Rebecca Brennan (10)
Holly Lodge Primary School, Ash Vale

School

The playground,
Fun, enjoyable, cool!
A place of freedom,
A slice of Heaven,
A concrete wonder,
The playground.

The classroom,
Boring, tiring, dull!
A place of imprisonment,
A section of Hell,
A brick disaster,
The classroom.

George Green (10)
Holly Lodge Primary School, Ash Vale

I Wish I Could Be A Sunflower

I wish I could be a sunflower
A sunflower I wish to be
If I were a sunflower
I could relax against a tree.

I wish I could be a sunflower
A sunflower I wish to be
If I were a sunflower
I could say 'hi' to a bee.

I wish I could be a sunflower
A sunflower I wish to be
If I were a sunflower
There'd be one big family tree.

William Petley (10)
Holly Lodge Primary School, Ash Vale

The Vampire Is Back!

Graveyards, blood and ghosts,
The things I love the most.

Bats flying overhead,
Swooping down among the dead.

People crying, laying graveside flowers,
Shall I go and haunt one of the church towers?

Expectantly I see some people - lots of flesh,
Hooray! Tonight I'll have something fresh.

You never know what's in store,
Beware, I may come and knock at your door!

Lauren Sweetman (11)
Holly Lodge Primary School, Ash Vale

The Sea

The sea
Like a world that sways
Mysteriously blue
Like the dreams I have in Cornwall.

The sea
Has many creatures big and small
But the dolphins I think are most
Wonderful of all
Like the dreams I have in Cornwall.

The sea
And all I have to do is
Walk into my bedroom
And there it is before my eyes
Like the dreams I have in Cornwall.

Bridie Mason (11)
Holly Lodge Primary School, Ash Vale

Computers!

Computers, computers
They're all the same; drive every adult completely insane.
But I've got the best one in the world.
It works 24/7, with no buttons to press,
My computer, it knows best!
I use my printer every day,
My printer it just purrs away.
I use it for homework,
I use it at home,
I use my computer when I'm all alone.
Now everybody has one exactly the same,
Everyone in the world now has a . . .
. . . *Brain!*

Laura Armstrong (10)
Holly Lodge Primary School, Ash Vale

My Worst Day At School

I was having a truly great day
Everyone had plenty to say.
After the film we charged outside
We ran like the wind far and wide.

Matt and I went running around
There was definitely a shortage of sound.
But suddenly I crashed, banged and fell
I really didn't feel very well.

I put my hand up to my head
And my sleeve suddenly turned red.
I wanted to go home to my bed
But mum called an ambulance instead.

When I arrived at the children's ward
I had a long wait and got so bored.
I knew I would have stitches in my head
My stomach was churning, my heart was lead.

After they had healed my head
They said I could go home to my own bed.
I felt as happy as I could be
I got to go home with my family.

Georgina Pedley (10)
Holly Lodge Primary School, Ash Vale

My Mum

My mum,
Always there when you need her.
Caring, honest and fun,
As cool as a dancing diva,
As loveable as a puppy,
I can trust her in every way.
She always makes me happy,
My mum.
I have a life of happiness!

Katie Hunt (11)
Holly Lodge Primary School, Ash Vale

Going Dancing

Getting ready for dancing in my pink leotard
Walking down the street
And waving and saying 'hello'
To everyone I meet.

I get into the Ash Community Centre
And all my friends are there
We start to play running
And my mum says, 'Take care.'

I get into dancing class
And do all my moves
Then I bend, stretch and twirl a lot
Next I leap like a deer with hooves.

When I start going home
Out through the door
I'm really freezing cold now
But then I go to the Budgen's store.

When I get home I watch TV
Then I think to myself that it was really fun
I turn on the lights
Though it is very bright like the sun.

Sarah Durbridge (10)
Holly Lodge Primary School, Ash Vale

Lions!

Lions,
Jaws biting, claws catching,
Petrifying, terrifying, scary,
Like a black hole with teeth,
Like a living nightmare.
They fascinate me,
Like Sylvester watching Tweety.
Lions,
Like a living puppet on a string!

Alexander Taylor (10)
Holly Lodge Primary School, Ash Vale

Fast Grow

I had a pup chow, as you know
I wondered if he would ever grow
He wanted a big fight
That went on through the night.

He started his jump
Over the big dog
The little dog started to grow
He didn't know where to go.

The dog finished his jump
Fully grown in a dump
I feel freaked out
The dog was about.

Then I woke up
He was a pup
It was a dream
I had to scream.

Charlotte Turner (9)
Holly Lodge Primary School, Ash Vale

Friendship?

Friendship,
Enjoyable until they let you down.
Fun, sad, spirit-crushing,
Like ripping out your heart,
Like destroying your soul.
I feel really sad about it,
Like wiping out all meanings of life,
Betrayal,
Reminding me you can never really know someone.

Gareth Downs (11)
Holly Lodge Primary School, Ash Vale

Snow

The snow
As white as paper
As white as the clouds
Melting as it hits your arm.

The snow
As cold as the Atlantic
As cold as the North Pole
Falling through the cold breeze.

The snow
As beautiful as a clear blue sky
As beautiful as the stars at night
Making a picture as you walk.

The snow
As dangerous as the white shark
As dangerous as a polar bear
The snow.

Amy Bollons (10)
Holly Lodge Primary School, Ash Vale

Bedroom Horrors

I feel
Icy breath on my skin
People
Under my bed making loud footsteps
-But it was just the rain outside.
The new babysitter making ghostly movements downstairs
Hot, sweaty
Chubby arms clenched around me
My little brother snoring in the background
Nightmares sweeping around my bedroom.

Emma Rance (9)
Holly Lodge Primary School, Ash Vale

A Day In The Life Of A Spit-Boy

I am exhausted, angry and tired,
But if I don't carry on I will be fired.
Dirty, starving and extremely hot,
Feeling miserable, staring at the pot.
Not allowed to move or even scratch my face,
Just to sit here in exactly the same place.
It's horrible being a spit-boy,
A life with no laughter, a life with no joy.

Sally Wood (10)
Holly Lodge Primary School, Ash Vale

A Spit-Boy

I do want to go to sleep
I do
But will they let me?
No!
If I do I will burn the food.

There are lots of good drinks for me
But I am hungry and tired.
Oh dear, oh dear.

Megan Kenny (9)
Holly Lodge Primary School, Ash Vale

The Whale

There was a racing driver from Ash Vale
Who raced in Monte Carlo in a gale
He said he was flat
But now he was fat
'Cause he decided to eat a huge whale.

Frederick Bragg (9)
Holly Lodge Primary School, Ash Vale

Spit-Boy

My arms are aching,
The turkey is roasting.

The fire is crackling,
The meat smells delicious.

I am hungry and thirsty,
I am tired and burnt.

The job's done for today,
Hooray, hooray!

Melissa Buxton (9)
Holly Lodge Primary School, Ash Vale

Rivers

Puddle
As I start to flow
I saw through the hard soil
I make my way down the mountain
I'm moving rapidly
I try to dodge the rocks
I have no control
I hit the bottom with a great splash
I slow down as my width grows.

John Rothwell (10)
Holly Lodge Primary School, Ash Vale

The Sumo From Ash Vale

There once was a sumo from Ash Vale
Who bought a weak boat and sail
He sailed away
But broke the next day
And ended up fighting a whale.

Steven Turnidge (9)
Holly Lodge Primary School, Ash Vale

Hide

There is an apple core
On the floor
It is really hard
And bumpy and a bit cold.
I can hear the crackling and popping
Of the fire bearing the wood
And sparks dancing.
It smells very smoky in here mostly
But sweet once in a while, you know?
It is really hot in here
But I will get used to it.
Oh no, it sounds like
Someone is coming down the hall.
Hide!

Emma Morley (9)
Holly Lodge Primary School, Ash Vale

Dogs

Pepper is funny
He likes his bum tickled
He dances.
Poppy likes her tummy tickled
She likes a hug from me
She gives me a wet and sloppy kiss
Pepper and Poppy love barking at the postman.
The doorbell rings, here they go, barking again
In the morning they scratch my legs off
When I go to school they sit on the window sill and say bye
When I come back from school they lick me
Poppy sits in the chair when I watch TV
I love Poppy and Pepper!

Sara Daborn (10)
Holly Lodge Primary School, Ash Vale

Rum Tum Tugger

(Together as a class we read 'Tum Tum Tugger' by T S Eliot and we wrote our own version during school. This is mine)

Rum Tum Tugger is a clumsy cat,
If you offer him a rat he'd rather be splat,
If you offer him to be splat he'd rather the rat,
If you give him Burger King he'd rather McDonald's,
If you give him warmth he'd rather a rat called Ronald,
If you give him Mickey Mouse he'd rather Donald,
Yes, the Rum Tum Tugger is a clumsy cat,
And there isn't any call for me to ignore it,
For he will do
As he do do
And there's no doing anything about it!

Lucy Dewdney (10)
Holly Lodge Primary School, Ash Vale

Spit-Boy

The meat is roasting,
It smells like a roast dinner,
Two hours passed, I'm almost falling off my chair.

I drink my beer,
While looking at the meat
And it looks like I want to eat it.

The smell is on its way over here
And it smells lovely,
My hands are getting burnt, crispy and black.

The fire is as hot as a sun or an oven.
It's very smoky.
After eight hours I finally fall asleep.

Stephanie Sherry (10)
Holly Lodge Primary School, Ash Vale

The Spit-Boy

I can hear people laughing,
Drinking as I turn the spit.

I wish I was Henry.
I wish I was Henry.

I felt sweaty and burnt,
My skin is peeling like paper, sweat is running down me.

I wish I was Henry.
I wish I was Henry.

My clothes are covered in grease.
They stick to me.

I wish I was Henry.
I wish I was Henry.

It's one o'clock in the morning,
Time to sleep.

Henry's dead.
Now I'm having a party and going hunting.
Then all of a sudden
Water hits me, back to work.

I wish I was Henry.
I wish I was Henry.

Jessica Townsend (10)
Holly Lodge Primary School, Ash Vale

Playground

Children do so many things
They run,
Skip,
Hop,
Jump.

You play games with each other,
You play hopscotch,
Stuck in the mud,
You do everything together.

You pretend you're as free as a bird,
You're a horse grazing in its field,
You pretend you're a happy family.
Children do so many things
It's a shame to grow up really.

Rowanne Steed (10)
Holly Lodge Primary School, Ash Vale

Spit-Boy

The flames were fun to watch flicker
My face became bright red
The clothes that I wore were old, dirty rags
We sometimes get to wear nice clothes
Looking at the wine made me thirsty
The meat made me hungry
All I got to drink was water
Being a spit-boy made me tired
I slept on the cold floor.

Hollie Louise Everist (9)
Holly Lodge Primary School, Ash Vale

Spit-Boy

I am just classed an adult
I'm just sixteen
It is burning where I work
My hands and side are burnt
Pain in my hands
My side has gone black
One hour's gone by
Two, three, four
I have finished.

My bed is itchy
Not at all comfortable but very warm.

I awake, it was just a dream
But this is my future.

Shelby Parker (10)
Holly Lodge Primary School, Ash Vale

Pocket Money

'Stack the dishes.'
'Why don't you do it?'
'Tidy your room.'
'Why don't you do it?'

'Take the dog out.'
'It's not my turn!'
'Take out the rubbish.'
'It's not my turn!'

Doesn't my mum know I'm still only ten?
Every time I refuse she threatens me,
'Do you want your £2.50?'
'OK. What else needs doing?'

Louis Manders (10)
Holly Lodge Primary School, Ash Vale

When On Holiday

I went to the children's disco,
Felt like a party babe, cool as cool can be,
But as the time was ticking on,
I began to feel nervous and shiver with fear.

He said, 'Megan, come up and sing.'
I said, 'No-o-o,' as my friends pushed me up.
I began to sing, my heart beat fast,
Was it me or the hotel dog howling?

I did not want to sing in front of thirty-five people,
With them all clapping like crocodiles' teeth,
I said, 'I am *not* doing that again,'
As my mum was saying I could not sing!

Megan Allen (10)
Holly Lodge Primary School, Ash Vale

An Old Person

There was an old person called Tim
His wife was nice and was called Kim
He bought a blue boat
He put on his coat
And he fell into a big bin.

He got out in a very big rush
He scrambled past a strange bush
He got in his boat
He started to float
He went home to his wife Kim.

Sophie Mansfield (9)
Holly Lodge Primary School, Ash Vale

Life As A Spit-Boy

I'm excited but nervous,
It's so hot and I'm thirsty!
I'm tired and hungry,
While I turn the spit all day long,
With nothing at all to eat!

I get hotter and hotter,
As I turn the spit all day long,
The meat is cooking and smells quite burnt!
I really want to eat it,
But can't, just can't!

Two hours pass,
I'm still so hot,
I am a zebra,
Nice skin one side, burnt the other!

I have to eat the meat,
It looks lovely and crispy,
I feel like I'm in a dream,
The smell is wafting through the kitchen,
So nice and smelly!

I'm in my old rags,
I'm still turning the spit,
I'm drinking all the beer,
I am nearly falling off my little wooden chair!
Ahh, good. Food's finished, time for tea!

Emily Cato (10)
Holly Lodge Primary School, Ash Vale

The Moon

The moon is a silver coin
In the pocket of a cloud.
It is a silver bauble
On the top of a Christmas tree.
It is a silver bubble
Floating through the world.

Abigail Lamberth (10)
Holly Lodge Primary School, Ash Vale

Winning The Hard Match

I'm waiting in the corridor
I can hear the crowd roaring
I walk out with my head up high
And my heart is beating, beating.

The whistle blows, I have the ball
Suddenly someone fouls me
It is in the penalty box
And my heart is beating, beating.

The referee's red card goes up
The sticker is moaning
He goes off in a big huff
And my heart is beating, beating.

I hit the ball with a huge belt
It goes in the left corner
I run to the Chelsea crowd
And my heart is happy, happy.

It's strange the match is over now
I walk back with my head up
We have won the hard match now
And my heart is happy, happy.

Michelle Pendleton (11)
Holly Lodge Primary School, Ash Vale

Under The Sea

The sea is blue and sparkly,
It's a scrunched up piece of paper.
The waves crashing against the shore,
There is glass shattered on the beach.

Underneath there's things to see,
Like fish, rocks, coral and me.
There are all sorts of fish with glee,
Don't forget the happy . . .
. . . dolphins.

Nicole Trevena (10)
Holly Lodge Primary School, Ash Vale

Horse Riding

When I went on holiday to Center Parcs
I went horse riding for the first time.
We had to go in a minibus to get there
To a lovely stable off the park in a nearby village.

When we got there I found myself standing
Waiting to get a hat.
Then we went to see our horses
And to be told their names.
Mine was called Bess.

She was black
Just like the horse in Black Beauty.
I climbed up steps to mount my horse
Then we went trotting into the school grounds.

We were standing in a line
Waiting to learn how to ride
First trotting around and then
We turned a corner to change our direction.
The horses were good
And now we had learnt how to stop.

I felt cruel the way we had to kick them
To make them walk on and on.
It was lunchtime and my horse was getting hungry
And it was kicking its feet and pulling its head forward
So I quickly got off and we all went back to the minibus
Which then took us back to Center Parcs.

Tamara Williams (10)
Holly Lodge Primary School, Ash Vale

Questions, Questions, Need More Questions

Is it hot?
Is it cold?
What is it like
To be bold?

Why are things high?
Why are things low?
What is it like to be
On a TV show?

Is it water?
Is it ground?
What is it like
To be in a pound?

Why are things fat?
Why are things thin?
What is it like
To be a pin?

Is it in?
Is it out?
What is it like
To be a Brussels sprout?

Why are things quiet?
Why are things loud?
What is it like
To be proud?

Hannah Queux-Johnson (10)
Holly Lodge Primary School, Ash Vale

The Stream

Spring,
Gets faster,
Smashes at the rock,
Trickles down the mountainside,
Passes the fluffy sheep,
Rushes past the tall, green trees,
Fish swim around in the clear water.

Flowing,
Past houses,
Cuts at the sides like a knife,
Rushes past the tall buildings,
Cows peacefully drink relaxingly,
It crawls into the village slowly,
People jump in playing happily.

Zakary McNamara (11)
Holly Lodge Primary School, Ash Vale

Chocolate

My mum says I can't have chocolate
Before my tea
So I scream and scream
And ask for no peas.

After tea
I ask for a chocolate sundae
My mum says, 'No'
So I go away.

I feel really annoyed
So I sneak into the kitchen
And say to my dog, 'Go away!
I want a chocolate sundae.'

Hanna Kelly (10)
Holly Lodge Primary School, Ash Vale

Black Beauty And Foal

As I gaze through the trees,
I see beneath the leaves,
A black beauty and foal.
I look slightly to the right and see an abominable sign
Saying this farm is to be sold.

Oh, that faulty black beauty and foal so small,
Going to just be left.
I must try my best, even if it means making a mess
To get them out of stress.

I run home to get some soft straw,
As I blunder in the door,
I got some money and left in a flurry,
For they are in need and so poor.

Sarah Neill (10)
Holly Lodge Primary School, Ash Vale

I Am . . .

. . . I am a bird.
I am a tree.
I am an aeroplane.
Look at me.
I am a dolphin.
I am a whale.
I am a snail.
Look at me.
I am mummy.
I am daddy.
I am *me!*

Charlotte McKeown (10)
Holly Lodge Primary School, Ash Vale

We're Goin' To The Beach

It's sunny today
We're goin' to the beach
Mum's gone to town to buy some bleach
Sam's playing in the sand with his bucket and spade
Granny's knitting in the shade
Granddad's eating a massive ice cream
Sam's paddling in a nearby stream
Dad's looking at the babes on the beach
Doesn't realise they are out of his reach
Boy, it's hot
I think I burnt my bot
Mum's on the phone
It's time to go home.

James Merryweather (11)
Holly Lodge Primary School, Ash Vale

Sand

Both liquid and solid
Black, yellow and red
Itchy and horrid
Yet
A soothing mud bed
As heavy as a trophy grand
Yet
As light as a spineless feather
Sand
The oldest type of leather.

Toby Scott (10)
Holly Lodge Primary School, Ash Vale

The Mars Man

I'm looking out the window,
I see a green-skinned guy,
He's really, really ugly,
And only has one eye.

He is staring right at me,
And I see his big nose,
He has got a dark red horn,
And he doesn't have any toes.

He's an alien from Mars,
He's in his cool spaceship,
He's visiting all the stars,
But his rocket has crashed,
And his engine is smashed!

William Batterbee (10)
Holly Lodge Primary School, Ash Vale

They Won't Get Me

Kicking, punching, pushing, shoving
Climb out of a hole and cry
I've seen his head in the toilet
I've seen his head in the bin
I'll run away
I'll disappear
They won't get me, they won't
I'll run like a greyhound
I know you've seen it too
Don't stay
Just run away
I know I will.

Larna White (11)
Holly Lodge Primary School, Ash Vale

My Folder

I dream a stream on my folder
It flows as it goes down the mountain
Trickles as it goes down the mountain
Hitting the rocks as it goes down my folder, my folder.

I dream a ballet dancer on my folder
She dances beautifully on my folder
Spins and twists on my folder
How charming she dances on my folder.

I dream of lots of things on my folder
How beautifully she dances
How the stream flows
But now it's time to work
So I dream . . .

Jade Woolfall (11)
Holly Lodge Primary School, Ash Vale

The Sea

Mermaids splash around the pearl rocks,
Dolphins leap beneath the waves,
The sea, the sea, the magical sea.

Turtles glide on the seabed,
Fish swim around the coral,
The sea, the sea, the magical sea.

Seaweed floats all around me,
While the blue whale passes by,
The sea, the sea, the magical sea.
The sea!

Magical!

Phoebe Leung (11)
Holly Lodge Primary School, Ash Vale

What Is The Sun?

The sun is a tennis ball
Flying through the sky,
It is a ball of gas
Hanging in the night sky.
It is a beach ball
Hanging in the night sky.
It is a flame of a match.
It is the start of a poem.

Adam James Kenny (11)
Holly Lodge Primary School, Ash Vale

The Blazing Sun

The blazing sun
Supplier of life
Flaming, shining, burning
As hot as a pressure cooker
As bright as a floodlight
I am grateful that it is there
It makes me feel as hot as a furnace
The blazing sun.

Matthew Debenham (11)
Holly Lodge Primary School, Ash Vale

Chocolate

Chocolate,
Sweet, brown, chunky!
Like a slice of Heaven,
Like a plank of fat,
For me, it's the key to life!
I feel like a lottery winner
Whenever I eat it.
Chocolate,
A world of happiness!

Laurence Thomas (10)
Holly Lodge Primary School, Ash Vale

White Fluffy Clouds

White fluffy clouds
They fly high above us
Soft, big, white,
Like a white boat on the ocean
Like a bird in a field
They make me feel happy
It makes me feel like I am in the sky
White fluffy clouds
But now the clouds must go by.

Carl Sherry (11)
Holly Lodge Primary School, Ash Vale

Matthew

He is eleven years old (it doesn't seem it)
Tall, big, fuzzy
He is as tall as a skyscraper
He is as thick as a twig
He reminds me of a tree
He makes me feel like a small ant.

Josh Williams
Holly Lodge Primary School, Ash Vale

What Is Green?

Green is a grasshopper,
As bright as a bouncy ball,
Like new green beans and lettuce,
And grass that's fresh and cool.

Green is the stems of flowers,
Apples, juicy and sweet.
Green is the eyes of black cats,
That you would like to meet.

Hannah Walter (11)
Mayfield CE Primary School, Mayfield

Dogs

Dogs can stretch
And dogs can prance
Dogs can dig
And dogs can bark
Dogs can laze
And dogs can play
Dogs can bite
And stay all day.

Matthew Sutton (10)
Mayfield CE Primary School, Mayfield

What Is Purple?

Purple is a tulip,
A mask in the perfect play.
Purple is a butterfly fluttering away.
Purple is a pen as lucky as the meeting.
Purple is a paint, it curdles when it's heated.
Purple is the purple heart upon the US Army.
Purple is a party where all the kids are barmy.
Purple is a colour across the whole known land.
Purple is a colour I hold in my hand.

Guy Bryan (10)
Mayfield CE Primary School, Mayfield

Somewhere In The Ocean Today

A hungry shark eagerly hunts for food
swimming in the dark gloom.

The shells are grazing on the bottom of the ocean
draining their beauty in the sand.

A clam clings onto its home
dreaming, dreaming if it will ever move home.

Georgiana Hall (10)
Mayfield CE Primary School, Mayfield

What Is White?

What is white?
Snow, pebbles, paper
it is nothing
a bland shade
a cold surface
an old sock you want to throw out
but if you really think hard
and shut your eyes
you will begin to make sense of it all.
It may be a dull colour but it is fun in the snow
and it is good writing on white paper
but then the bad thoughts come into your confused head.
White is the colour of a bullied child
a severe illness
and then death.
White is a very confusing colour
since it represents so much.

Caspian Kingdon (11)
Mayfield CE Primary School, Mayfield

Glasses

Wicked glasses,
round glasses,
looking-very-geeky glasses,
oval glasses,
square glasses,
slipping-off-your-nose glasses,
sunglasses,
fun glasses,
bend-them-any-way glasses.

Jack Chapman (10)
Mayfield CE Primary School, Mayfield

What Is Black?

Black is a smoky bonfire,
The cold, dark, haunting colour of death.
Black is as black as a horse's tail,
Sprinting through a green meadow.
A huge, black bat taking over the night sky
After he disappears.
A cold, lonely and sad colour,
The only colour left in the crayon box.
Black is a smell of burnt toast.
Black is the colour of pepper,
The colour of a computer screen,
That has been left on . . .
As scary as the Devil's stare.

Alice Lambert (10)
Mayfield CE Primary School, Mayfield

What Is Brown?

Brown is the slow drip of chocolate ice cream.
A bubbly puppy, the crispy leaves running from it.
Brown is a staring cloud lashing out silently.
Brown is a sweet perfume clinging for ever.
A tree trunk swaying free.
Brown is a *snap!* of milky chocolate.
A wandering feather.
A brown, slinky cat.
Brown is the strong smell of cocoa that greets you in the morning.

Paige Waterhouse (11)
Mayfield CE Primary School, Mayfield

What Is Red?

Red is a sly fox,
slinking around the woods.
It's a grinning, fat Santa,
eating Christmas puds.

Red is freshly drawn blood,
dribbling down a sword.
It's a colossal heart full of love,
that shall always be stored.

Red is sun-drenched roses,
that sprouted from a seed.
It's a big pair of bulging lips,
waiting to feed.

Red is furious anger,
flared nostrils spurting steam.
It's a little robin in the sky,
looping in the sunbeam.

Red is sweet strawberries,
juicy as you bite.
It's a field of glorious poppies,
creating a memorable sight.

Red is boiling hot cheeks,
embarrassed to show his work.
It's a lovely bush of berries,
where people like to lurk.

Tommi Caldwell (11)
Mayfield CE Primary School, Mayfield

My Hamster

They sleep all day
and play
at night
but when they get up
they give you a fright!
Mine's two and half
really quite old.
If he gets
any older
he might go bald!
His teeth
are quite sharp.
If he bites me I squeal!
He makes loads of noise
whizzing round
in his wheel.
His name's Cappuccino,
he's ginger
and white.
I love him
although
he wakes me up
in the night.

Joel Brummer (10)
Mayfield CE Primary School, Mayfield

I'm Going Topsy-Turvy

I went to the paper shop this morning,
And bought a magazine last night.
I ripped it up then read it,
Then I went to bed and turned on the light.
I slept with my eyes open,
Ate breakfast with them closed.
Then once I was at school
I answered a question wrong and got it right.
Then we did maths,
I wrote a poem
And then came English
I did a sum.

Nicholas Kent (11)
Mayfield CE Primary School, Mayfield

What Is Gold?

Gold is a warming
colour of winter light.
Gold is a bold colour
showing might.
Gold illuminating
up luxurious lights.
Gold is a pirate's delight.
Gold is the sunset
burning bright.

Max Ward (10)
Mayfield CE Primary School, Mayfield

Somewhere In The Ocean Today . . .

A shoal of scaly fish glide delicately through the turquoise water.
Exploring divers excitedly search out an old, green-covered
    shipwreck not touched before.
Reassuringly, dolphins launch their tails high above from the
    deep ocean.
An echoing sound promises company is near.
Smooth, shiny rocks lie on the surface of the golden sand.
Lonely seaweed strands slither letting their slimy skin leave them.
Swallowing hard, navigators truthfully see a large boat zooming
    towards them.

Francesca King (10)
Mayfield CE Primary School, Mayfield

In The Sea Today

In the sea today
the fish are rushing
through the battered driftwood
glistening in the sunlight.

The sun is beating down
on my head.
A gentle breeze is blowing on my face.

Fishing boats seem to be
falling off the edge
of the world.

Henry Noakes (10)
Mayfield CE Primary School, Mayfield

What Is Red?

Scrumptious
strawberries
ruby red,
ruby lips
overfed!
Red is angry
hot and strong
chilli peppers
smooth and long.
Blood tomatoes
squashed into
ketchup.
Love and
passion in
a bottle.
A red rose
is love on
a stick.
Fit for
a king
to give to
his queen
or just
to give
to you.

Joshua Rimmer (11)
Mayfield CE Primary School, Mayfield

Through That Door

Through that door
Is a field of unicorns
Soft and silky
With their tails waving in the morn
Where they prance through
Grass and flowers
Having fun for hours and hours.

Through that door
Is a land of magic
Where enchantment flows - *wow!*
Here anything can make
All your dreams come true!
And especially made for you
To wish you luck in all you do.

Through that door
Is a land of elves
Where lovely flowers grow
They get a spade
And in they delve (looking)
Digging potatoes from their rows
And in the evening when time has come
There'll be a lovely dinner from your mum!

Alexandra Weager (8)
Potley Hill Primary School, Yateley

Rebecca O'Flanagan's Leaving School

Rebecca O'Flanagan's leaving school,
She's leaving our school for good.
She doesn't want to leave our school,
And would stay if she possibly could.

Rebecca O'Flanagan's leaving school,
Her family are moving house.
At school Rebecca was very quiet,
As quiet as a mouse.

Rebecca O'Flanagan's very clever,
She knows her alphabet.
She's been tested on it so many times,
And never got it wrong yet.

Rebecca O'Flanagan's leaving our school,
I think it's a big, big shame.
She may no longer be with us here,
But we'll always remember her name.

Charlotte Dale (9)
Potley Hill Primary School, Yateley

Jousting Tournament!

I am a knight, a fearsome knight,
I ride my horse as fast as he goes,
I fought my way to the final,
I won some horses and trophies,
I am a champion.
I have done some stunts to avoid lances,
Ducking and dodging,
I steer my horse with speed and agility,
Some men have died, some survived but fell from their horses,
I will enter jousting competitions and hopefully get through.
I am *the* champion.

Alexander Allen (9)
Potley Hill Primary School, Yateley

Sea

I love to think about the sea
It's such a pleasant place to be.

And if I lived inside the sea
I think a dolphin I would be.

I'd swim and swim and dance and play
And I would do this every day.

I'd dance and play around with friends
But would we find the sea's end?

I'd dance and play all night
To live like that, oh what a delight.

And if I lived inside the sea
I think a dolphin I would be!

Ellie Conroy (9)
Potley Hill Primary School, Yateley

Lost

Lost,
Never found,
Searching forever,
For the soul of a traitor,
You have to dig deeper,
To find the heart of a robber,
Who has stolen another's,
It is easy to find the pain in a sufferer,
Who tries to find,
The soul of a traitor,
The heart in a robber,
Which is,
Lost.

Laura Payne (9)
Potley Hill Primary School, Yateley

Winter

Winter's so nice with snow and ice
And puddles of frosted water.

Winter's coming.
Winter's coming.

Santa's here, let's all give a cheer
And watch the reindeer fly.

Winter's coming.
Winter's coming.

Winter's so dark, there's snow on the ground.
Look in the trees, leaves can't be found.

Winter's here.
Winter's here.

The children get sledges and away they go.
Listen to the laughter from the snow.

Winter's going.
Winter's going.

Spring's coming.
Spring's coming.

Lewis Trower (10)
Potley Hill Primary School, Yateley

Tiger

The tiger is sleek
The tiger is disguised
In the grass
Is where it lies
Ready to pounce
On unwilling prey
He has many a victim
That will come his way.

Laura Hesketh (11)
Potley Hill Primary School, Yateley

Countries At War

People come in boats
And they don't even get on the beach
They die on the boat by getting shot.
Some people die and some people don't.
People run over grenades and blow up.
Some get injured and some don't.
Helmets filled with blood
When men put them on
Blood goes on their heads.
When the men get home
They are pleased to see their families.
They go to a funeral
Some cry
Some don't.

Nathan Connolly (7)
Potley Hill Primary School, Yateley

Friends

Friends are great.
Friends are fun.
Friends help you when you feel glum.

They make you laugh.
They make you cry.
They make you want to touch the sky.

Friends are nice.
Friends are funny.
Friends help you spend all your money

Sana Haseeb (7)
Potley Hill Primary School, Yateley

Fireworks

On the 5th of November all over the land
We celebrate what Guy Fawkes planned!
Up in the sky, into the night
Fireworks explode so big and bright.
Some are red, some are green
The prettiest you've ever seen.
Some are purple, some are gold
That makes you forget you are so very cold.
Some go bang, some make a snap
As the bonfire burns you hear it crack.
You must be careful and stay safe
Then wait until next year to enjoy it again.

Thomas Still (9)
Potley Hill Primary School, Yateley

Hope

My treasure stretches out beyond long paths of existence,
It lurks around undusted corners,
Banished from view of sight,
As it secretly yarns the golden thread that is never-ending,
The thread runs through all,
Some find it deceptive,
As it clears each debris of our lives,
For each and every soul.
What is my hidden treasure?

The gift of hope.

Sophie Crisp (10)
Potley Hill Primary School, Yateley

Who Am I?

I am tail light.
I am small and fluffy.
I live in a cage.
People hug me and kiss me.
Lots of people love me.
I am very light.

Who am I?

A cat.

Bethany Rosier (8)
Potley Hill Primary School, Yateley

Ghost Street

She walks around the midnight street
All around her a ghostly screech
She looks about but nothing's there
So she stands alone in the cold night air

All the houses turned to sleep
Except for one down that ghostly street
She wonders what is happening there
Thinking alone in the cold night air.

She opens the door and tiptoes in
Finding creepy noises are within.
She trembles up the creaky stairs
Scared, alone in the cold night air.

Along the landing, through the door
She wishes she could see no more
A gush of wind ruffles her hair
Whirring, in the cold night air.

An ice-cold hand touches her shoulder
She turns to see and she is no longer.
She had become death, standing there.
Now she was the cold night air.

Jenni Wilson (10)
St John's College Lower School, Southsea

As Time Goes By

Mum is cleaning Dad is working
Things around me are evolving
People changing is a way of life
No matter what happens so be it if I die
I will always have my family by my side forever.

Sisters almost all grown up
Don't know where time has gone
One day they too will leave home
Live your life to the full just as I will
Girls do not worry for I will be there.

Parents are old
Lived their life too the full
Had a comfy life to share with other people
To enjoy just the same
As I will some day
But for the mean time I am here to stay.

Parents are close what a life they have had
I'm a proud father just like my dad
My children are well and so is my wife
Just if my dad had the time to see what a boy can grow up
To be just like me.

My time is close no reason to stay I am just on death's door
Children have moved
Just like I will up to a place of the best.

Kristoffer Yeomans (11)
St John's College Lower School, Southsea

A Big Fat Bug

There once was a big fat bug,
Who lived in a big fat jug,
He used to chase the spider
Who drunk a lot of cider
That funny, ugly jug bug.

Jonathon Forer (11)
St John's College Lower School, Southsea

Nature's Seasons

Autumn
Leaves turning brown and falling
Crisp, crunchy layer on the ground
Squirrels collecting nuts
Ready for the big sleep
Days becoming shorter flowers fade away
Weather turning cold.

Winter
Trees stand bare against the grey skies
Ground white with snow
Birds gone away
Animals sleep
Shortest day is here
Weather crisp and cold.

Spring
Grass turns green again
Buds burst, colours appear
Sleepy animals awake
New lambs leap in the meadows
Days getting longer
Weather warmer.

Summer
Birds singing from dawn to dusk
All around brightly coloured flowers
Farms preparing for harvest
Golden corn swaying in warm breeze
Longest day is here
Weather is hot and dry.

Clare Langhorn (11)
St John's College Lower School, Southsea

Castaway

The wind billows around a lone sail moving along the horizon.

The sand light underfoot
The waves crash and bash, tumbling to reveal
                                    the world's mountain-scapes.
The cliff quivers as it loses an unsettled battle with the sea
It's pummelled,
Crumbles under the order of Poseidon's domain.
A seagull fights an unseen enemy that goes by the name of the wind.

A storm cloud looms in the ominous grey sky
A beam of light shines through the night illuminating rocks and boats.
The rain lashes down upon all in its path.
The wind screams like a lost soul, dying.
A flare of lightning reflects upon the mountainous waves.
A thunderclap resounds upon the cliffs and in the caves,
                                    a signal to the storm to break mayhem.

The morning dawn soothes the lowly battle
The sun rises where she fights a duel with the fleeing clouds and,
Victorious,
The wind dies down as if the lost soul has been settled.
The rain ceases its patter; all is quiet
The Himalayan sea becomes the smooth Arctic snow,
Never moving
Still.

The lone sail silhouetted on the horizon continues its travels.

Emily-Jane Randall (11)
St John's College Lower School, Southsea

Dragon

Any man who is strong and brave,
Shall ride on a horse to the darkest cave.

There he will find a beast with powers,
But when he meets him he always cowers.

With slanting eyes he looks so fierce,
With long, sharp claws he can pierce.

His body is huge, hard and scaly,
He has a diet of humans daily.

As he glides over church and spire,
He lets out a roar while breathing fire.

He's magical, mythical, have you guessed?
A dragon of course, they are the best.

Louis Cook (10)
St John's College Lower School, Southsea

Silent Space

Space is a place
With planets around.
It's so big
There's not even a sound!
Except for the rumbling rockets that roar
Do you think there's a sound?
I'm not sure.
There's the stars that shine and twinkle
And not even the sound of the *Piggiwinkle!*

Sylvain Wear (7)
St John's College Lower School, Southsea

'Quack!' Said The Billy Goat

'Quack' said the billy goat
'Oink' said the hen
'Miaow' said the little chick
Running into the pen.

'Hobble gobble' said the dog
'Cluck' said the sow
'Tu-whit tu-woo' said the donkey
'Baa' said the cow

'Hee-haw' said the turkey
'Moo' said the duck
All at once the sheep went,
'Cock-a-doodle-doo!'

The owl coughed and cleared his throat
And he began to bleat.
'Bow-wow' said the cock
Swimming in the lake.

'Cheep cheep' said the cat
As he began to fly.
'Farmers been and laid an egg -
That's the reason why!'

Hannah Collis (8)
St John The Baptist CE (Controlled) Primary School, Southampton

The Jungle

The jungle is very noisy and big,
There are animals all about,
The trees are very big and stout,
Offering a play area and habitat for all about.

Monkeys are very cheeky,
Tigers are very sneaky.
The jungle is very creepy.
Wouldn't you like to have a peep!

Megan Watts (8)
St John The Baptist CE (Controlled) Primary School, Southampton

Aaahh Rug!

When Mum bought the rug
It was cosy and snug
But when Mum was out
It moved about.

Rug came alive,
And began to thrive,
On our front door,
And loads, loads more.

When Mum came back,
And saw the mess,
It all came down to me,
I had to confess.

But what to tell,
Of the white fluffy rug,
That used to be cosy,
Warm and snug.

Would Mum believe me?
If I should say,
'That fluffy white rug
It came alive today'?

So the very next day,
When Mum went out,
The rug began to scream,
Curse and shout.

I took it in my arms,
And shoved it down a drain,
I don't know how I did it,
But I never saw it again.

Abigail Puttock (11)
St John The Baptist CE (Controlled) Primary School, Southampton

The Splats

It's a funny thing that a chewing-gum splat
Should lay by the side of the street.
All blotchy and grey and messy like clay,
Sticking to people's feet.

And a splat's best friend is a cigarette end,
Thrown carelessly on the floor,
They're rolling around on the cluttered ground,
Sprawling outside a shop door.

One time the street was tidy and neat,
The pavement was clean and bare.
Now it's littered with yuck and all kinds of muck,
By people who couldn't care.

The human race would have a smilier face.
If only people would see,
That no more litter makes this place fitter,
For people to live in, to be.

Jessamy Tucker (11)
St John The Baptist CE (Controlled) Primary School, Southampton

Solomans Lane

My name is April
I live down the lane
I love living here no day is the same
Plenty of mates to play in the park, I would stay until its dark,
Ohh we love horses, tomato sauces, sunny days and country ways
Clip-clop on Saturday morn, wakes me in a tired yawn,
Dog dying for a walk
Sunday roast and family talk
Ohh we love horses, tomato sauces, sunny days and country ways.
It is great living in the lane
I never want to move again.

April Palmer (7)
St John The Baptist CE (Controlled) Primary School, Southampton

Kittens

Kittens big, kittens small
Kittens climbing up the wall
Kittens cute, kittens fat
But my kitten is a cat.

My cat is big but it is small
What is it I call?
It is a small kitten,
Wearing a mitten.

My cat has grown even more,
He scratches and scratches with his claw
Down by the wet water my cat is by the river.
Come home, come home and don't you shiver.

It is done but it was fun
Telling you about my cat Tom.

Daisy Chester (9)
St John The Baptist CE (Controlled) Primary School, Southampton

Volcano

The volcano shaking its angry fists
Spitting out fire like a dragon
Rushing down like a bull
Its hair was flaming red.

Its voice booming like a giant
Spitting lava in the sky
Like a firework high on high
Its eyes beaming red

Suddenly it goes silent
It's not booming or beaming
No more spitting lava
It has gone to sleep.

Eleanor Shepherd (9)
St John The Baptist CE (Controlled) Primary School, Southampton

The Angry Volcano

Bubbling softly,
In a silent mood,
Completely contained
In a quiet room.

Rising, rising,
Up and up,
Pressure, popping
At the top.

Hotter and hotter,
Boiling over,
Sizzling angrily,
Bang!

Slowly, slowly,
Creeping down,
Burning anything,
On the ground.

Hissing, spitting,
Crying out loud,
Bubbles popping
Not a sound!

Edward Gaffney (10)
St John The Baptist CE (Controlled) Primary School, Southampton

Senses At The Seaside

As I lay on the sandy shores
I can hear seagulls squawking
And the children laughing
I can hear the sea lapping against the rocks with a mighty force.

As I eat my sandwiches
I can see sails drifting away in the distance
I can also see boys surfing and girls sun bathing

As I paddle in the shallows
I can smell salt from the sea
And chips from the arcade
Freshly made sandwiches in children's hands.

As I bury my toes in the sand
I can taste my ice cream
And the salt from the sea
I can also taste the odd bit of sand in my sandwiches.

As I lay under the sun's rays
I can feel the sand between my fingers
And the sea rippling over my toes
I can also feel the shells under my hands.

Fay Sebborn (11)
St John The Baptist CE (Controlled) Primary School, Southampton

The Moon And The Stars

The moon is a glow in the sky,
It follows me everywhere,
The stars twinkle and flicker
Like a thousand torches.

The moon does tricks
The clouds cover the moon.
Sometimes it is like a teddy
Sleeping in the palm of my hand.

I love the stars they are with me all the night.
The moon and stars make me feel safe,
They tell me I am close to my family
When I am travelling home.

Kimberley Martin (8)
St Mark's CE Primary School, Farnborough

My Best Friend

My best friend is silly every second
But then she eats flies
That's why she is silly.

When I am sad she is my hero,
She would fly up and fall down (and do her funny show dance)

When I go round her house. I call her silly, but her nickname is Millie
So she calls me Silly Millie.

Each day at school we play at our sneaky,
$\qquad$ silly club and do silly things at break.

Lauren Gray (7)
St Mark's CE Primary School, Farnborough

Colours

The brightest colour is yellow
The colour of a corn meadow,
Colourful.

The darkest colour is black,
The colour of a steam train running down the track,
Colourful.

The blankest colour is white,
Like a ghost giving you a fright
Not colourful.

The happiest colour is green
The colour of a sick football team,
Colourful.

The sportiest colour is red,
The colour of a painted sport shed.
Colourful.

The saddest colour is grey,
The colour of a wolf eating his prey.
Colourful.

Dylan White (7)
St Mark's CE Primary School, Farnborough

Vic

Vic was neither smart nor dumb
But his belly busted buttons.

Vic was not ugly or lovely
But he had a huge bushy beard

Vic was not hot or cold
Vic was dead

Vic was not kind or mean
Vic was a *Viking!*

Andrew Sanderson (9)
St Mark's CE Primary School, Farnborough

Animals

The largest animal must be whale
Looking for a jumble sale.

The smallest animal must be an ant
A lot, lot smaller than an elephant.

The meanest animal must be a shark
Looking for a place to park.

The kindest animal must be a rabbit
With a weird habit!

The fastest animal must be a cheetah
And he's a very good beater.

The slowest animal must be a tortoise
Always losing his races.

Max Dawber (8)
St Mark's CE Primary School, Farnborough

Food Groups

The world is full of foods I know
Pickle, onion, pepper.

The world is full of foods I know
Burgers, egg, fish.

The world is full of foods I know
Bananas, apples, grapes.

The world is full of foods I know
Cheese, yoghurt, butter.

The world is full of foods I know . . .
I wonder when tea is?

Connor Woodhams (7)
St Mark's CE Primary School, Farnborough

Sportsmen

If you are Tim Henman
You play tennis all the time
But if you are not him please
Don't hit the ball over the line.

If you are Jonny Wilkinson
You are training all the time
But if you are not him please
Put the ball over the try line.

If you are David Beckham
You wear football boots all the time
But if you are not him please put
The football over the goal line.

If you are Darren Campbell
You are running all the time
But if you are not him please
Put your foot over the finish line.

Joshua Smith (9)
St Mark's CE Primary School, Farnborough

Animals Big And Small

The largest animal in the world must be
The elephant whisking his tusks through the trees.

The tallest animal in the world must be
The giraffe flicking his neck from side to side at me.

The smallest animal in the world must be
The ant creeping all over me.

The loveliest animal in the world must be
The dolphin splashing in the sea with me.

Olivia Farrell (9)
St Mark's CE Primary School, Farnborough

Scary

There is a haunted house in a
Graveyard.
Scary,
Scary.

In the haunted house there's
A cobwebby organ.
Scary,
Scary.

In the haunted house there's a
Tall Frankenstein.
Scary,
Scary.

In the haunted house there's a
Singing ghost.
Scary,
Scary.

In the haunted house you can
Hear the trees whistling.
Scary,
Scary.

In the haunted house you can
Hear a boy
Screaming.
Scary,
Scary.

Maisie Gowers (8)
St Mark's CE Primary School, Farnborough

Pearl Harbour

7th December 1941
It was early in the morning
The ship jolted as through it had been hit by
A wrecking ball.
Alarms rang like church bells
It was the Japanese.

Midday mayhem
Everyone was on deck helping
Fires had spread across the boat.
White figures with red dots flew over us.
The Arizona spreading like leaves

An unexpected defeat
The air was filled with the clatter of machine guns
Bombs fell like rocks.
Suddenly the tides turned,
The Japanese were in full retreat.

Christopher Seargent (8)
St Mark's CE Primary School, Farnborough

Animals

Animals are like pets
Animals have vets,
Animals can be in the sea,
Animals play with me,
Animals can fly,
Animals can spy,
Animals eat food,
Animals can be rude,
Animals can run,
Animals are fun!

Melina Mukherjee (8)
St Mark's CE Primary School, Farnborough

Cute Kittens

Kittens are such beauties
And they're such small cuties
With their soft, silky fur
And rounded ball like eyes.

Their tiny, little paws
And their razor-sharp claws
Are their dangerous back up.
One be one they're sharpened
On the bouncy blue couch.

They look cute and cuddly,
But not all are.
They scamper and creep
To find a treat
Like a bird in a tree or a tiny mouse.

If you come across a furry kitten,
Don't have thoughts about picking it up
And taking it home
Because your house won't be a pleasure dome
After that kitten's done with it.
It'll be messy and ruined,
Covered with feathers,
So watch out and keep your eyes peeled!

Rachel Harrison (9)
St Mark's CE Primary School, Farnborough

Butterflies In The Summer

S ilent butterflies fluttering by
U nbelievable colours shimmering in the sun,
M unching leaves in high branches,
M oving their transparent wings through the air.
E verywhere butterflies,
R ivers of amazing butterflies.

Tierney Martin (9)
St Mark's CE Primary School, Farnborough

In The Jungle

In the wet jungle
The alligator is lurking in the marshy swamp.

In the cold jungle
The spider is shivering whilst the wind brushes past his web.

In the silent jungle
The tiger is watching and waiting for his prey.

In the wooded jungle
The monkey is swinging from vine to vine, branch to branch.

In the lonely jungle
The snake is slithering through the tall grass.

In the hurt jungle
The hunters are chopping down animals' habitats and killing them.

Zoë Woodhams (9)
St Mark's CE Primary School, Farnborough

All Animals

A jaguar is black, like a lump of mud.
A jaguar's footsteps are like tiny raindrops splashing on the floor.

A charging rhino is rough and tough, like a car smashing into a wall.
A rhino has rough skin, like coal in a fire.

A bear is furry like the fur on a cactus.
A bear is strong like Ray Mysterio the wrestler

A parrot is as colourful as a picture on a wall.
A parrot's feet are as sharp as a knives.

Adam Arden-Smith (8)
St Mark's CE Primary School, Farnborough

Spirits Of Times

Sometime ago a Roman emperor had everything,
A dog, some gold and soldiers for defence.

But he did not defend himself,
Meanwhile he planned to conquer the world.

Some prisoners overheard them
Planning to conquer the world

The prisoner escaped and went to Europe
Where he got some terrifying British soldiers.

The English stayed to defend.
The Romans charged at Europe and defeated them.

The English were defeated.

Jordan Wrigley (9)
St Mark's CE Primary School, Farnborough

The Strangest Animals

The fastest animal in the jungle must be
A panther running around, trying to catch his food.

The slowest animal in the jungle must be
A snake slithering around the branch of a tree.

The stripiest animal in the jungle must be
A tiger hiding ready to jump out.

The toughest animal in the jungle must be
A gorilla swinging from tree to tree.

Todd Cave (8)
St Mark's CE Primary School, Farnborough

10 Toppings On A Pizza

The spiciest topping on a pizza must be
pepperoni with its outside ring.
The sweetest topping on a pizza must be
pineapple in little square chunks.
The sauciest topping on a pizza must be tomato puree like glue.
The juiciest topping on a pizza must be
pepper with its three different colours.
The tastiest topping on a pizza must be
melted cheese like a big blanket.
The chewiest topping on a pizza must be ham as pink as candyfloss.
Let's just say pizza is delicious.

Rebecca Howard (8)
St Mark's CE Primary School, Farnborough

Forest

In the dark and bushy forest
A stripy tiger standing under the hands of a tree.
Like the witch's fingers making
A potion.

The tiger's tail is like a stripy smooth snake
Gliding through the grass.

The grass is waving in the warm air.
The branches hide the tiger from the hunters
Trying to get the coat.

Jessica Read (9)
St Mark's CE Primary School, Farnborough

My Bicycle

The tiniest sound my bike makes must be
The steering of the handlebars

The loudest sound my bike makes must be
The screeching of the tyres.

The happiest sound my bike makes must be
Its bell, ringing across the road.

The funniest sound my bike makes must be
The pedals with their chain sounding like my dad snoring.

The best thing about my bike is
When you get up in the morning
You can play with it.

Sam Duckhouse (8)
St Mark's CE Primary School, Farnborough

Concorde

As the roar crumbles
It lifts like a peregrine falcon
Zooming up.

As the engines burn
It zips up like a flash of lightning
At high speed.

As the speeds drop
It simmers down like a feather falling
From a nest.

Daniel Ibbott (9)
St Mark's CE Primary School, Farnborough

Animals I Like

I like elephants
They have a wrinkly trunk and they squirt water.

I like tigers
They have black stripes, the biggest roar you have ever heard.

I like giraffes
They have a long neck, brown spots, they munch green leaves.

I like monkeys
They eat bananas and swing from tree to tree
A bit like me.

Olivia Richmond (7)
St Mark's CE Primary School, Farnborough

Sounds

The fastest sound in the world is a zooming
Concorde flying through the air.

The slowest sound in the world is a turtle
Crunching across the beach.

The noisiest sound in the world is a lion roaring
Through the jungle.

The happiest sound is the sun rising
In the morning.

Jacob Crossley (8)
St Mark's CE Primary School, Farnborough

The Sweet Countryside

Far, far away from here,
A field has been laid down,
Sweet, green grass,
And a hill so brightly shown.

On that hill, far, far away,
On the field that has been laid down,
Flowers are brightly coloured,
And a flock so brightly shown.

On that hill, far, far away,
On the field that has been laid down,
Bright, tall, bushy trees,
And a cottage prettily shown.

On that hill, far, far away,
On the field that has been laid down,
It's a large, wide countryside,
Plain, long countryside,
That hill, far, far away . . .

Joanna Phillips (8)
St Mark's CE Primary School, Farnborough

Creepy Noises

The wind is a howling wolf
Screeching round the world.

Lightning is a broken bulb
Flickering and flashing in the sky.

Thunder is a roaring tiger
Crashing in the jungle.

Shane Gurney (9)
St Mark's CE Primary School, Farnborough

Cars

The silver shiny rims and
The red metallic spray paint,
On the racing car.

The black strong bumper and
The speedy spiked tyres,
On the racing car.

The noisy new engine and
The hard mighty brakes,
On the racing car.

The amazing reflecting windows and
The smoky, gleaming exhaust pipe,
On the racing car.

Matthew Stilwell (8)
St Mark's CE Primary School, Farnborough

Watching Cars From My Window

Watching cars from my window
Silver cars like raindrops moving quickly,
Gold cars like the sun shining brightly,
Green cars like grass swiftly swaying in the wind,
White cars like a cloud rushing across the sky,
Blue cars like the sky hovering above us,
Watching cars from my window.

Myles McLean (8)
St Mark's CE Primary School, Farnborough

Sea Otters

In the Pacific Ocean, sea otters live,
Sea otters float and sleep on their backs.

They are endangered animals, dear oh dear,
The poor sea otters are in fear.

They sleep on their backs in the black night sky.
Teaching their babies when the morning has come.

The babies are learning how to swim,
But a baby called Kym learned how to swim and . . .

She got tangled up in a fishing net,
It was a trap for her to be a pet.

Poor old Kym dead in the net,
But Mum and Dad are still getting wet.

Megan Jousiffe (9)
St Michael's CE Primary School, Playden

Elephant

The small baby elephant walks on the dry, dusty floor,
While the sun closes its big yellow doors.
His mother comes and they watch the sun go down.

The little baby elephant cuddles his warm mother.
The mother gets some palm leaves to cover up each other,
They did not know it was their last cuddle together.

As the sun rises up again.
Poachers came and took his mother's ivory,
He watches sadly his mum go away.
Suddenly a few drops come from the baby elephant's eyes.

Jackson Woodcock (9)
St Michael's CE Primary School, Playden

Snow Leopard

Once there was a snow leopard
Called Rageo.
He lived in a snowy cave
Every week he had his afternoon bathe in the snow pit.
The walls of the cave were very tall
He would crawl along the floor
To the entrance of the cave
To go for a adventure
It was very cold in his dimension.

He smelt something in the air
Something told him it was coming from over there.
He ignored the smell and walked straight on!
But there was a poacher in sight called Tom.
Tom got up and grabbed his gun.
And Tom said, 'This is fun!'
Bang! went the gun
As fast as the wind.
Poor dead Rageo
Waiting to be skinned.

Martyn Smith (8)
St Michael's CE Primary School, Playden

Lion

There once was a lion in the jungle
He had four friends and they tumbled
All over each other, they are really good mates.
Little did they know what was their fate.

They were being followed by hunters.
They went to drink
But the river was poisoned
Poor little lion dead on the floor.

Dewi Bowen (8)
St Michael's CE Primary School, Playden

Nelly

Nelly was my friend
Until he went around the bend
He lived out on the plains you see
And had one knobbly knee.

But because he had this knobbly knee
Hunters got his ivory
And that's when he fell to the ground
And after that he was never found.

And now poor Nelly has gone away
And I have no friend to run and play
I guess this has been my unlucky day
All I can say is Nelly has gone today.

Tom Nunn (8)
St Michael's CE Primary School, Playden

Orang-Utan

The happy family swing from tree to tree
Then the little one said, 'See see!'
The night sky was light
The stars so bright

The baby orang heard the shot.
The baby orang fell from her cot.
Then the baby orang was taken away.
This was the end there would be no more play.

The baby orang was caged and sold.
She would die lonely and not very old.

Alex Blumire (9)
St Michael's CE Primary School, Playden

The Tiger Poem

There were some tigers that jumped in glee
But all of the poachers they did not see
No tigers except one did realise
That tiger ran to avoid the cries
The tiger ran in the forest green
To all parts he'd never seen.

This tiger's name was Stripey Terry
His life until now was very merry
He did not want to be in the market sale
He wanted to avoid all that wail
Stripey Terry liked his home
But he did not like being on his own.

Suddenly there was a man with a gun
Poor Stripey Terry couldn't see in the sun
It really really hurt
He wasn't alert
I will never forget Stripey Terry
His coat was as red as a cherry.

Freddie Scott-Cracknell (8)
St Michael's CE Primary School, Playden

All About Polar Bears

One day in the Atlantic there was a polar bear
She lived on an iceberg floating everywhere.
Catching fish for supper in the frozen sea
Swimming, playing, alive and free.

Polar bears are furry, very, very fluffy
Poachers coming to skin the polar bear for coats
Leaves the polar bear to suffer.

Alissia Mathews (7)
St Michael's CE Primary School, Playden

Baby Orang-Utan

A baby orang swings to his mother.
They get up close and cuddle each other.
They get all comfy and use each other.
As a lovely comfy cover.

They didn't hear the hunters coming
They didn't hear the footsteps drumming.
The bushes started to shake.
The orang started to quake.

The hunters slowly climbed up the tree.
They grabbed the baby orang and pulled her down.
Her mother turned around, she was not there.
She didn't know where she was.
She was sad.

Charlotte Blumire (7)
St Michael's CE Primary School, Playden

The Sad Whale

There once was a whale that lived in the sea
With his mum, his dad and his brother (me)

We loved our lives in the sea to that day
Then poaches with masks took it away.

They took all our blubber and turned it to oil
And was put in a pot to sizzle and boil

They broke up our home, they broke it up bad
And we'll never have the home that we always had.

Alfred Lloyd-Dyke (9)
St Michael's CE Primary School, Playden

Siber The Endangered Tiger

There was a tiger
Who's name was Siber
He lived in the jungle
All in a tumble
He went out hunting one fine morn,
The next thing he knew he was gone.
He was on a boat large and wide,
He was trapped! On a boat large and wide.
He felt really sick he really did,
A man pushed him into a cage he really did.
Siber the poor tiger passed away.
He wasn't seen any other day.
Now let's just say never hunt
Or they'll be no animals even no elephant.

Oliver Dickinson (9)
St Michael's CE Primary School, Playden

Baby Koala

This little baby koala is call Maisy,
This little baby koala is very lazy.

She lived in the eucalyptus trees,
And ate lots of leaves.

Maisy's home was chopped down by men in green coats,
The trees were shipped out by river on boats.

Maisy sat all alone,
No food to eat and no home.

Tanya Beckett (9)
St Michael's CE Primary School, Playden

The Koala Called Tiny Jack

The koala lives in the outback,
In a eucalyptus tree,
Then the koala called Tiny Jack,
Saw that his mother was going to be
Kidnapped in an old brown sack.

The mother was getting some food for them,
The hunters were spying on her,
Then the mother was put in an old brown sack
And they tied it up with a rope,
And took her away from the outback.

Charlotte Kingham (8)
St Michael's CE Primary School, Playden

Panda Poem

Baby panda cuddles his mother
All wrapped up in the tree cover.

All safe and sound
Hoping not to be found.

Creeping through the bushes, a man with a gun
Deep in the shadows, out of the sun.

The man shot the baby panda mother
The baby panda ran out of the tree cover
Before he was shot too.

Lauren Clark (8)
St Michael's CE Primary School, Playden

What Is . . ?

What is the earth?
The earth is a bowling ball
Slowly heading towards the gutter.

What is a helicopter?
A helicopter is a chainsaw
Ready to strike.

What is an earthquake?
An earthquake is a motorcar
Crossing the busy roads.

What is a plane?
A plane is a bird
Soaring across the sky rapidly.

David Blackie (10)
Shinewater Primary School, Langney

What Is . . .?

What is a kitten?
A kitten is a lively jack-in-the-box
Popping up everywhere.

What is the Earth?
Earth is a giant marble
Rolling around the world.

What is a snowflake?
A snowflake is a young cat
Nudging you with its nose.

Eleanor Davis (10)
Shinewater Primary School, Langney

What Is . . .?

What is a kitten?
A kitten is a sleeping baby
Lying on your lap not making a sound.

What is a plane?
A plane is a flying carpet
Letting you travel wherever you want.

What is a snowflake?
A snowflake is a butterfly
Which lands gently on your hand.

What is a ghost?
A ghost is the howling wind
Floating in the air waiting to scare you.

Katie Cain (10)
Shinewater Primary School, Langney

Shark

I, king of the sea,
Speed through the ocean
And study the waters of my land
For any living prey.

I, king of all fishes,
Control the weak water creatures
Like they are my slaves.

Those pathetic fishes are all feeble and weak.
Not even one of those tiny things
Could defend themselves.
No wonder they are my prisoners for eternity.

Jack Brookes (11)
Shinewater Primary School, Langney

Ape

I, king of the apes
The mightiest of all,
Hate those two-legged animals
Capturing us for zoos.
Well, I have had enough
One of these days they will pay.
They hardly give us food.
Why?
Cos they are jealous of all the apes.
If only I and all my apes
Could get out of these prisons.

If only I was a two-legged animal
I would be disgusted with myself.
I wouldn't walk out of the door.

They will bow to me!

Alexander Lawson (10)
Shinewater Primary School, Langney

Dragon

A ferocious dragon
Releases fiery breath
Death-defying, invincible, mythological
Like a fire-breathing griffon,
Like a giant flying volcano.
I feel terrified
Like a chicken waiting to be roasted
A ferocious dragon.
I know I will never be able to win the battle to survive.

Charlie Milner-Heels (10)
Shinewater Primary School, Langney

Falcon

Ready to take-off,
That's me, king of the sky
Grasping my catch,
Piercing its flesh into the bone.
Ready for take-off
Vanquishing my prey
Digesting it in one day.
Ready for flight
Soaring through the sky,
Getting the bird's eye view from up high
Better not come onto my turf or you'll die.
Ready for sleeping
This is my day,
But tomorrow I'll continue with the same
Although now I lay
I conjure up another plan for catching the meal of the century!

Jamie Long (11)
Shinewater Primary School, Langney

Dragon

Dragon
Terrified of nothing or no one.
Petrified, enormous, ferocious.
Its fire is like boiling lava erupting from a volcano
The dragon's teeth are as sharp as a dagger.
I feel frightened
I'm so scared that I'm shaking
Like a bomb about to explode.
The dragon.
Makes me feel like another victim
About to be swallowed whole.

James Houston (10)
Shinewater Primary School, Langney

Huntback Turtle

I, the huntback turtle,
A skilled and talented creature,
Can live to tell the tale for a hundred years or over.
I am the rarest turtle of all.

My precious shell
Lies upon my restless back
No one disagrees that my shell is the best.
Clearly I am the best turtle of all.

As I waddle and paddle in the sea
My heart just beats faster and faster
I am the king and I will reign for evermore.

Emily Mackie (10)
Shinewater Primary School, Langney

Dragon

A dragon
A fire-breathing barbarian
Bloodthirsty, violent, brutal.
Like a meteorite burning down to Earth
Ready to destroy.
Its breath is like a ray from the sun.
I fell purely weak
Like a small and powerless ant
A dragon, the sun,
Red and indestructible.

Sophie Kiteley (11)
Shinewater Primary School, Langney

The Marvellous Dolphin

I am the marvellous dolphin
Don't race me at swimming - I'll win!
The bottlenose breed I am,
I attract men with my looks,
They see me in the wildlife books!
I battle sharks with my strength,
My skin is soft and cuddly.

I am the marvellous dolphin
The cute, attractive dolphin.

I am the eye-catching dolphin,
I gulp down nutritious fish,
I don't devour them on a dish!
My eye is a jet-black marble
My gleaming teeth are pointed like needles.
I'm sympathetic to the human breed,
The water shoots out of my hole like a fountain.

I am the marvellous dolphin,
The cute, attractive dolphin!

Daniella Meredith (10)
Shinewater Primary School, Langney

Cobra

I, the cobra, the almightiest creature ever,
Slither around my jungle kingdom
I search for prey.

I wrap myself round an innocent monkey
To have for my supper.
I ravel myself up, pretending to be asleep.
But I am watching my prey.

Andrew Tickner (10)
Shinewater Primary School, Langney

Monkey

I, monkey, king of the jungle
Swing from branch to branch,
Protecting my land from prey and intruders.

I, sovereign of all monkeys,
Have everything I desire
Although the humans still think they rule us.

I will change that sooner or later,
Soon I will rule humans and all jungles.
I will not have to bow down to them.
They will bow down to no man but me.

Michael Wratten (10)
Shinewater Primary School, Langney

A Screaming Tornado

A screaming tornado
Spinning so fast you get sucked up,
Rotating, twirling, petrifying.
Like a Hoover making earth clear
Like a drain sucking water.
I feel terrified
Like I'm being chased by air.
A screaming tornado.
Makes me feel I'm a victim about to swallowed.

Gabrielle Whitaker (10)
Shinewater Primary School, Langney

What Is A Snowflake?

A snowflake is an angel
Descending from Heaven
It never travels alone
And it brightens up the darkest depth.

Paul Feeney-Cooper (10)
Shinewater Primary School, Langney

Computer

A computer
A mind-beating machine,
Superb, intelligent, powerful.
A clever human trapped inside plastic.
A human inside, reading and learning.
I feel like human brains have been beaten.
Computers are alive.
A computer.
Makes me realise that computers are ready
                        to get revenge on humans.

Luke Warner (10)
Shinewater Primary School, Langney

Thunder Cinquain

Thunder
The floor trembles
With a very big bang
Like a monster walking around
Scream, scream.

Kellie-Marie Griffiths (10)
Shinewater Primary School, Langney

The Ocean

Crashing and splashing, twirling and spinning.
Whirling and whinnying as if it were singing.
It lashes out at me as I stand upon the beach,
But as it tries and tries to get me I'm way beyond its reach.
I tease it and tease it again and again.
But then a mighty roller takes me from the sand in which I have lain.

Jack Webb (10)
Skippers Hill Manor Preparatory School, Five Ashes

Enemies

I - the lonely wanderer through the dark night
I - the peacemaker who can stop a fight.
I calm the storms and stop the waves.
I battle with the bad and the good I save.

You - the evil spirit of the ferocious sea.
You - if only You could turn my force into We.
You power the weather and sway the trees,
When you could still the storm and restrain the leaves.

Jessica Thomson (11)
Skippers Hill Manor Preparatory School, Five Ashes

Mountains

Mountains
White with snow
Enormous! Brilliant! Dazzling!
Like a white curling snake,
Like a tower pointing to the sky.
I feel awed
Like I'm staring up into the heavens
Mountains
Reminds us how small we actually are.

Holly Ellis (10)
Skippers Hill Manor Preparatory School, Five Ashes

In Wintertime

In wintertime
When snow comes down
Amid the once-green grass,
We sit inside,
Around the fire,
Just like the winter last.

Will Johnson (10)
Skippers Hill Manor Preparatory School, Five Ashes

I Can See

I can see the ground.
I can see the sky.
I can see so far down low.
And I can see up high.

I cannot see wind,
I cannot see air
I cannot see birds
When they're flying way up there.

I think I can see dragons,
I think I can see knights,
I think I can see monsters
They always give me frights.

In a way I can see love
In a way I can see hate,
In a way I can see hope,
In a way I can see fate.

I hope I will see Heaven
I hope I won't see Hell
For Hell is full of fires,
Yet Heaven rings with bells.

James Barnes (11)
Skippers Hill Manor Preparatory School, Five Ashes

Stars

Golden stars beautiful things
Burning high in the sky
Lighting up forests
Lovely things are stars
But then they disappear
But they will come back tomorrow
At night.
Mysterious things are stars.

Louis Catliff (8)
Skippers Hill Manor Preparatory School, Five Ashes

The Sleepover

Mum shouts, 'Time for bed,
You sleepyheads.'
'Oh,' we moan
And whine
And groan
We lollop and slump up the stairs,
Not even bothering to say our prayers!
Mum has gone up to bed,
Why should we?
We'll have a feast instead.
'I'll get the chocolate,
You get the sweets.'
'Gosh this will be a really nice feast!'
'Oh no! Oh bother, my brother's awake!
Go back to bed for goodness sake.'
Phew he has gone,
So let's carry on.
Goodness gracious get back to sleep,
My mum is coming to have a sneaky peek.
We've had no sleep
The sun is rising,
To tell you the truth
That's not surprising.

Jessica Arnold, Naomi Brown (10) & Jenny Goodwin (11)
Skippers Hill Manor Preparatory School, Five Ashes

Chocolate

Oh chocolate what a joy, it slithers
Down your throat like a snake
What a taste it is, oh!
Could eat it every day
I can't swallow it
For the taste is
Exquisite!

Natasha Howie (9)
Skippers Hill Manor Preparatory School, Five Ashes

The Dentist Chair

I sat in the
Dentist chair
Looking left
And right
The dentist came
In
Looking very bright
Trying to keep
My
Teeth
Tightly shut
Looking scarily
At him
Keeping my
Eyes shut
Here comes that
Drill I thought
Clutching
To my
Teeth
Oh no I
Thought
I need a
Single
Sweet!

Samantha Hedley (8)
Skippers Hill Manor Preparatory School, Five Ashes

Cat Poem

There are all different types of cats
There are some cats that even wear hats
Some cats are furry and soft
Some cats are rough who sleep in the loft
Some cats are lazy who sleep all day
Some cats are active who like to play
Some cats are naughty and tear sofas apart
Some cats are good and are very smart
Some cats are crazy and mad
Some cats are boring and sad
But no matter what type of cat they are
I still love them all even if they sleep in my car.

Olivia Dorman (10)
Skippers Hill Manor Preparatory School, Five Ashes

Leopard

The wind is a leopard
It bounds through open land.
And ruffles my hair
Their bite rips through my skin
Causing me agony
And both run fast
They make noises.
And can go anywhere
Up mountains too.
It makes my heart beat faster.

James Wood (8)
Skippers Hill Manor Preparatory School, Five Ashes

The Mermaid

Her hair is black as night,
Her lips as red as blood,
Her eyes like a torch so bright,
That's the hour when she brings rain or flood!

Her beauty makes nature look bad,
The flowers that sit in her hair,
The moonlight that lights up the water,
Reflects on her face so fair!

Among the coral rocks,
She larks beneath the waves
Enticing ships towards her,
To meet their watery
Graves!

Emma Christmas (9)
Stone Cross Primary School, Stone Cross

Dogs

Dogs are furry, dogs are great,
I have one that is my mate.
When my cousin comes around to play,
He always tells him to leave,
But I tell him . . .
'He's not doing anything, now don't tease!'
In his bed a dirty towel,
I don't know why he likes to prowl.
He is dirty, he is messy,
But most of all he is so squirty!

Will Mitchell (9)
Stone Cross Primary School, Stone Cross

If It Weren't For Dad

If it weren't for Dad I'd
Turn up my music,
Turn the TV over,
Turn the volume up,
Put a DVD in,
Play in my room all day,
Stay at home,
Give him a doll baby,
Give him a D+ in school,
Make an ugly statue of him,
Give him a pet rat or mouse,
Give him a hammock to break,
Give him a smelly cake,
Take his mobile off him.

Otis Jarvis (8)
Stone Cross Primary School, Stone Cross

What Is Pink?

Pink is a dress
Pink is a hair bobble
Pink is a pig
Pink is a blancmange with a wobble.

Pink is fluffy
Pink is a rose
Pink is paint
Pink is blossom when the wind blows.

Lucy Murphy (9)
Stone Cross Primary School, Stone Cross

My Jelical Poem

Jelical cat sleek out of sight
Jelical cat sleek past at night
Dancing prancing all around
Dodging dogs on the ground.

They can climb up a wall
They spring through trees all
They scale the drainpipe
Into alleys they swipe.

Their long fluffy tails
That twitch in the dark
When you tread on his foot
He'll sing like a lark.

Charlotte Reynard (8)
Stone Cross Primary School, Stone Cross

My Birthday List

On my birthday list there is . . .

A PlayStation 2,
A kiss from the coolest boy in school,
A swimming pool,
A stack of money,
A year supply of honey.
A mobile phone,
A big ice cream cone,
A chocolate house,
A pet mouse.
I think that's it,
Nothing else in my head,
Aha a four-poster bed.

Vanessa Gatward (9)
Stone Cross Primary School, Stone Cross

This Is The Theme Park

This is the theme park where we went for a day.

This is the theme park where we went for a day,
And went on a high-speed roller coaster.

This is the theme park where we went for a day,
And went on a high-speed roller coaster,
And a relaxing Ferris wheel.

This is the theme park where we went for a day,
And went on a high-speed roller coaster,
And a relaxing Ferris wheel,
And a slow monorail.

This is the theme park where we went for a day,
And went on a high-speed roller coaster,
And a relaxing Ferris wheel,
And a slow monorail.
And a soaking wet log flume.

This is the theme park where we went for a day,
And went on a high-speed roller coaster,
And a relaxing Ferris wheel,
And a slow monorail.
And a soaking wet log flume.
And now I'm really exhausted.

Jacob Bradbrook (9)
Stone Cross Primary School, Stone Cross

Rabbits are . . .

R abbits are fluffy and cuddly
A nd I like them very much,
B ut they can sometimes be a bit messy,
B ut they are also very cute.
I like them so much I wish I had a dozen,
T o all the rabbits in the land, I love you all so much.

Jessica Lees (9)
Stone Cross Primary School, Stone Cross

The White Horse

Up on the top of the hill,
There lives the white horse
It is as white as snow,
It is lovely, it has silver eyes,
It has strength like the wind,
Very, very strong,
And very, very cold,
She's never moving, standing there looking still
She will stay forever.

Sophie Holyoake (8)
Stone Cross Primary School, Stone Cross

My Dog Is . . .

M y dog is kind to everyone
Y ou would like her

D oggy bones and treats
O ur dog is lovely
G uess her name . . .

It is Molly.

Lara Standen (9)
Stone Cross Primary School, Stone Cross

Dolphins

Dolphins are cute
Dolphins are cuddly
Dolphins can jump really high
Dolphins act in shows,
They are so clever
Dolphins are my favourite animals
I wish I could have a pet one.

Laura Jones (9)
Stone Cross Primary School, Stone Cross

Snail

'Snail upon the wall
Have you been silly at all?
Can you tell me?'
'Only this my child -

When the sun is hot it's all I've got.

The wind blows me away,
Like a butterfly
I don't know if you would like it.'

Sofie Gown (9)
Stone Cross Primary School, Stone Cross

Troubled Tilly

Troubled Tilly, troubled Tilly as bony as an escaped prisoner!
Her fur is like an electric wire spiralling out of control!
She switches herself on and off like you do when turning
on the television!
Woof, woof, woof! Tilly's voice is like a powerful megaphone and when
she barks it's louder than it seems!
Troubled Tilly, no not troubled Tilly, Tilly in trouble!

Jessica Graham (10)
Stone Cross Primary School, Stone Cross

The Mail Lady From Israel

There was a young lady from Israel
Who was always delivering mail,
She knocked on the door,
As her bottom was sore,
And found she had grown a tail!

Paul Stevens (9)
Stone Cross Primary School, Stone Cross

The Boy Who Lived

There was a boy named Harry Potter
Who's favourite animal was an otter.
He went to a place called Hogwarts School,
Where he acted cool - but not like a fool.
Harry hated a man called Professor Snape,
Who wore a horribly greasy cape.
He had a godfather in the prison of Azkaban,
And he didn't get as much as a tan.
Harry had the latest wand.
That he used to push Draco into a pond.
Voldemort tried to steal the Philosopher's Stone,
But in the end, he didn't have a bone.
And that's the boy who lived.

David Stevens (9)
Stone Cross Primary School, Stone Cross

My Fave Things

Jelly beans, cats, chocolate, Christmas.
Easter, my birthday, Mum and Dad and the sun.
Lollipops, allsorts, weekends, purple, gold.
Lipstick, money, bank notes, rainbows.
Yo-yo, stamps, glitter, gel pens, March.

Being called 'cupcakes' (and eating them)
And there are more: terrapins, flowers.
Balls, fish, stars, heart, hamsters.
It really is a lot; videos, PlayStation.
Eating salt and vinegar sticks, learning about cats.
Spyro, having good dreams, cola.

Catherine Holloway (9)
Stone Cross Primary School, Stone Cross

TJB Hamster

T JB is such a great friend always there for me.
J arec hates him but I think he is crazy TJB is lovely.
B ut if he could speak he would be the best in the world.

H e is so amazing how he carries food, he puts it in his cheeks and
the way he explores the world!
A m I crazy? No I love him so much that I made him a maze.
M y hamster oh, oh what should I do to make him happy
S o do you like hamsters or not?
T ry to work out what I will be when I am older and help me do it!
E very second, nature is being destroyed because man is
killing them for food!
R eally we must stop them or it could destroy man for food!

Tarran Basham (9)
Stone Cross Primary School, Stone Cross

I Went To The Zoo

I went to the zoo,
At exactly half-past two,
It was amazing,
I saw everything
From the fierce lion,
To the scaly python.

I went to the zoo,
And met a kangaroo
I do love animals,
Just like bulls.
I liked the swish of the tiger's tail,
And also a slimy snail,
I was too tired after being at the zoo!

Lily Gatward (9)
Stone Cross Primary School, Stone Cross

Beautiful Butterflies

B eautiful butterflies in the sky
U nder the branches that are so high
T he one and only butterfly
T he pollen floats in the sky.
E mbarrassment
R osy wings
F or the man to catch the lady's eyes
L adies dance every night
Y ou and I are a couple of butterflies.

Poppy Mallows (9)
Stone Cross Primary School, Stone Cross

Excuses, Excuses

Sorry Miss
I'm late
My hamster
Flew away on
A plate!
I tried to catch
It with my mate.
But my hamster
Landed in a steak!

Connor Rowan (9)
Stone Cross Primary School, Stone Cross

Earthquake

I can destroy nations in a single moment,
Or tear buildings in two.
With a flash of my anger I can be terribly lethal,
Sending terror across the land.
When calm I just
Disappear.

Peter Bray (11)
The Butts Primary School, Alton

Cold

I can make people shiver,
I can freeze up the river,
I can mist up all the windows and doors,
I can frost all the walls and floors.

I can lay down flat,
So you'd better keep on your hat!
I can freeze you like an ice block,
I can come in your home without having to knock.

I can come through the keyhole of your house,
You won't know I'm there, I'm as quiet as a mouse,
I can race with the breeze,
I can fly to a tree and it will lose all the leaves.

I flow through a tap and run on your finger,
There you will watch me slowly linger,
I am not pink, I am not blue,
You will not see me, I am see-through.

Ana Chambers (10)
The Butts Primary School, Alton

Snow

I can cover the land
In my soft, woollen blanket.

I silently fall
White as a lamb.

I race to the ground
I don't stop to hesitate.

I arrive when I want
I am never late.

I'm a danger when I want to be
I'm a one-season game.

I'm a Christmas spirit
Snow is my name.

Louise Datchens (11)
The Butts Primary School, Alton

My Magic Box

(Based on 'Magic Box' by Kit Wright)

There will be in my box . . .
A flick of a book from an old lady,
A drip from a tap,
A blink from a wizard.

There will be in my box . . .
A song from a bird,
A swing from a door,
A munch from a giant.

There will be in my box . . .
An old, ancient teacher's voice,
A dog's bark,
A swimming costume from a St Lucian man.

There will be in my box . . .
A wizard's house,
A crocodile's tail
And railway sleepers.

My box is fashioned from . . .
Sunflowers' petals
And bark of a tree,
Hinges are made of chicken wire.

I will jump in my box
On a bouncy trampoline,
As fast as a car
And bounce as high as a skyscraper.

I will swim in my box
In the Atlantic Ocean,
Above some sharks,
Hammerhead sharks.

Jon Bailey (9)
The Butts Primary School, Alton

Joy

Joy was her name
Paralysed she was
Watched the lottery
Every Wednesday and Saturday night
With her eyes half closed
Squinted at the television
She had friends and hope
No movement.

A sudden thought
A flashback
A sudden pain in her bones
Growing bigger and bigger
Remembering how her husband died in a fire
Just sat there alone
Thinking about it
As the pain faded away
Until nothing
Felt lonely
Thought she was mad
It seemed it
Lonely and sad.

Joy
Watching the lottery
Every Wednesday and Saturday night
With her eyes half closed
Squinted at the television
Joy
Heart of hope.

Emma Spooner (10)
The Butts Primary School, Alton

My Magic Box

(Based on 'Magic Box' by Kit Wright)

There will be in my box . . .
A miaow from an old cat,
A chirp from a robin,
A nut from a dead squirrel,
And an eye from a witch.

There will be in my box . . .
A tick of a grandfather clock,
A wash from a big wave,
And a breeze from a windy day.

There will be in my box . . .
A suck from a whirlpool,
A slam from a door,
And a cry from a baby.

There will be in my box . . .
The first tear from a street man,
The first sight from a blind man,
And a twinkle from a star.

My box is fashioned with gold,
With diamonds on the lid,
Witches' fingers for hinges
And lined with silver inside.

Michael Barwick (9)
The Butts Primary School, Alton

Fun

F is for friends and having fun
   it's even better when we can play in the sun.

U is for you and me
   we're as happy as can be.

N is for new things to do and play
   all the way through the day.

Shaun Barrett (7)
The Butts Primary School, Alton

Magic Box

(Based on 'Magic Box' by Kit Wright)

In my box there will be . . .
The fur from a white unicorn,
A scream from the first queen,
A bite from a romantic dinner.

In my box there will be . . .
A sparkle from the biggest diamond,
An acorn from the first oak tree,
The last tear from a mum.

In my box there will be . . .
Three magic words spoken in Japanese,
The first laugh from a carnival,
A glistening tooth from a baby.

In my box there will be . . .
A cheer from a race,
The snap from a ruler,
A trunk from a tree.

My box is made from . . .
Silver, plastic and crystal
With hearts on the lid
And wondrous wishes in the corners.
Its bottom is the collection
Of dinosaur bones.

I shall swim in my box . . .
Over the St Lucian island
And watch over the people that play.
I shall fly over the sunniest beach
And pick nice seashells.

Katie Pearce (10)
The Butts Primary School, Alton

Love

Her name was Love,
She was a deaf woman,
Each and every night,
When the moon came out,
She would come right into our house,
With her arms full of faith,
Walking along the perishing floor,
She'd had hope and doubt.

Then into the dark,
She came,
I saw,
Through the glazing corridor,
In and out the doors,
Her heart full of sorrow,
She made no conversation,
Why did she do that?
I wondered alone,
Not needing any comment,
Nor any welcome,
For she could not hear.

Love,
Each and every night,
When the moon came out,
She would come right into our house,
With her arms full of faith,
Love,
Friend of the spoken life.

Imogen Hoare (10)
The Butts Primary School, Alton

Joy

Joy she was named.
The little widow.
Saw her at the market
Every fortnight
With her head bent down
Wrapped up in a shawl.
Lonely and sad.
No love.

And then
I remember
A wave of sorrow
Swirling through a broken window.
Her distressed eyes gazing up darkly.
Twisting his wedding ring around her thumb.
But why?
Why didn't she leave it all
In the past?
Needing none of it
To find happiness
On her own.
Pleasure wouldn't find her.

Joy.
Saw her at the market
Every fortnight
With her head bent down
Wrapped up in a shawl.
Joy
Heart of love.

Ellie Callow (10)
The Butts Primary School, Alton

Joy

Joy, her name was
The sad woman
Took her to St Michael's Church
Every Wednesday evening
To the service
Nothing much
No husband.

Abruptly
I recall
A cold night in November
The loneliness was immense
In the graveyard
No light in the church
No sound
The bitterness of the cold was disturbing
She left all the happiness in the church
All the confidence in the past
But faith in the future
Boy
You'll never walk alone.

Joy
The sad woman
Took her to
St Michael's Church
Every Wednesday night
To the service
Joy,
Heart of gold.

Ben Spoors (10)
The Butts Primary School, Alton

In My Box . . .

(Based on 'Magic Box' by Kit Wright)

In my box I have got . . .
A bounce from a tiger,
A smile from a newborn baby,
A shimmer from the first piece of snow.

In my box I have got . . .
The biggest petal from a lily,
The first tear from a baby,
The brightest bit of light.

In my box I have got . . .
A smell of fresh roses,
A flitter from a butterfly,
A miaow from a cat.

In my box I have got . . .
A flicker from a hot fire,
A drip from the bluest river,
A bang from a gun.

My box is made of the tint
From a rainbow with pieces
Of snow on the lid.
Its hinges are diamonds.

I shall fly in my box . . .
Over the Atlantic Ocean
And watch the tide go in
And everyone go home.

Dominique Butler (10)
The Butts Primary School, Alton

The Funfair

The funfair, what shall I play?
Popcorn and sweets
What shall I say?
How about the haunted house?
Hip hip hooray!

The funfair, the funfair
What shall I do?
What about a swing ride?
And some candyfloss too!
How about the dodgems?
Hip hip hooray!

The funfair, the funfair
What shall I say?
How about the mirrors?
They will be OK.
I see a clown.
Hip hip hooray!

The funfair, the funfair
What a good day!
Oh, look, *a big, big, big slide*
Hip hip hooray!
And one for luck
Hip hip hooray!

Millie Anderson (8)
The Butts Primary School, Alton

Joy

Joy, that's her name,
The lady who is paralysed,
I help her to her armchair each night,
With her chair squeak-squeaking,
On the tiled floor,
Family and friends,
No movement anymore.

Suddenly I remember,
Noises round the market,
Hustling round the stall,
Walking through with her bag,
And sat down in a chair,
She could move back then,
No movement then,
She wanted some,
To move around,
Into the armchair I helped her,
Then turned the television on.

Joy,
Helped her into her chair,
Each night,
With her chair squeak-squeaking,
On the tiled floor.
Joy,
Heart of movement.

Joshua Browne (9)
The Butts Primary School, Alton

Magic Box

(Based on 'Magic Box' by Kit Wright)

In my box I will put . . .
A whisker of the first kitten born from a litter,
A roar of a leopard sleeping in the shade of a tree,
The first step taken steadily by a foal.

In my box I will put . . .
The first squawk called by a parrot,
A flutter of a fairy dancing in the moonlight,
A wing from the most wonderful butterfly.

In my box I will put . . .
A feather from the most magical bird,
The first twinkle from a star,
A bark from an old dog.

In my box I will put . . .
An eagle swooping down to catch a mouse,
A monkey swinging from the vines in a jungle,
A bright yellow petal of a sunflower.

My box is covered in ferns and leaves,
The mermaid scales on the lid
And dancing in the corners.
The hinges are snowflakes glistening.

I will sleep in my box
On a silk bed fit for a queen
And stay there until the break of dawn,
Then collect more things for another magical box.

Sophie Ilsley (10)
The Butts Primary School, Alton

Faith

Faith her name was.
The girl who wheeled the old man home
Each Wednesday night.
With his wheelchair rattling and clattering
Along the cobbled street.
He had a love for life
And a sense of humour even though he could not walk.

And suddenly
The old man fell into a trance
As the girl wheeled him home.
A tear slowly drifted down the old man's face.
The girl asked him what the matter was.
He said nothing.
He sat there so long saying nothing.
The girl sat down beside him
Stroking his hand gently.
They both sat for hours and hours
Staring into the fire.

Faith
The girl who wheeled the old man home
From the pub each Wednesday night
With his wheelchair rattling and clattering
Along the cobbled street.
The old mad had a love for life.
Faith
Heart of life.

Hugh Wallis (10)
The Butts Primary School, Alton

I Am

I am a doctor.
I wonder if I can save people?
I hear people scream and cry.
I see blood and broken bones.
I want to save people.
I am a risk-taker.
I pretend I am a professional.
I feel in pain.
I touch chemicals.
I worry about me failing.
I cry when I don't succeed.
I am a doctor.
I understand my job.
I say I am a professional.
I dream I pass my exams.
I try to fix bones.
Sometimes I fail.
I am Henri *Best.*

Henri Best (8)
The Butts Primary School, Alton

Sid The Slithery Snake

Sid liked Sidney the spider.
They liked to play snakes and ladders.
Sid liked to slide down the snakes.
Sidney sprinted up the steep ladders.
Sid and Sidney slid on their sledge.
They used a shiny spade to make a silly snowman.
Sid pretended to be a soft, stripy scarf.
Sidney pushed the slippery sledge with his super, sprinting legs.
He sprang onto the sledge and slapped right into the silly snowman.
Smash!
The friends were scrunched but safe in the soft snow.

Cameron Lockie (7)
The Butts Primary School, Alton

Grace

Grace she was,
The small, deaf woman,
Stayed in her little flat in London,
Watching television in her armchair,
Looked up to the sky,
Hearing unknown.

Abruptly,
I remember,
A wash of emptiness,
Rearing up through the open door,
No sound from the television,
Doesn't need to be,
She loved all who let her,
Needing nothing to help her,
She would say,
'I see glimmers of hope.'

Grace she was,
The small, deaf woman,
Stayed in her little flat in London,
Watching television in her armchair,
Grace,
Heart of hope.

Owen Smith (10)
The Butts Primary School, Alton

Tornado

A sudden twirl of anger, destruction,
Ripping through everything in its path,
A monster from within, evil as ever,
Dark as sin.

A stampede of rage, sadness,
A typhoon of power, strength,
People flee as if it is a bison of mass destruction,
A train of terror rattling on and on.

Nathan Lockie (10)
The Butts Primary School, Alton

My Magic Box

(Based on 'Magic Box' by Kit Wright)

In my box there would be . . .
A horn from the last unicorn,
A tooth from the fiercest dragon,
The wings from a fly.

In my box there would be . . .
Juice from the first ever coconut,
A fin from the oldest dolphin,
A ray from the sun.

In my box there would be . . .
A slice of the moon,
A slab of the first ever metal,
A string of hair from a cat.

In my box there would be . . .
The colour from the rainbow,
Three stars from the sky,
A piece of glass.

My box is made from darkness and light,
Mars is on the lid and magical dust on the joints.

I shall fly on my box into the mist of time
To collect the last items.
Then it will be perfect.

David Barrett (10)
The Butts Primary School, Alton

Blink!

Blink, blink again,
What did you miss in those seconds?
The flap of a bird's wing,
The drip of a tap,
The crash of a wave on the sand,
A leaf falling to the ground,
A baby's breath,
The wag of a dog's tail,
The pitch of a ball,
The flicker of a flame.
Blink, what did you miss?

Clarissa House (10)
The Butts Primary School, Alton

Frost

I can cover the land
In my crisp, icy layer.

I come in the night
Like Santa when I sleep.

I lie on the ground
My icy fingers crawl across it.

I arrive when I want
I am never late.

I'm a danger when I want to be
I'm an ice skater's dream.

I'm a winter visitor
Jack Frost is my name.

Maddie Joint (11)
The Butts Primary School, Alton

The Flood

Dark grey clouds gather,
They rumble with anger,
Suddenly a flash of light,
The sky seems to crack,
The ground trembles as the thunder crashes,
Raindrops fall, gentle at first,
Faster and faster,
Until long, sparkling rods fall from the sky,
Water gushes down the drains,
The river rushes, lapping at the banks,
Mud slips away and the water begins to creep,
Silently heading to a lonely little village,
Sparkling rods get shorter and shorter until . . .
The rain stops,
Dark grey clouds are chased away by fluffy white sheep,
The sky lightens up and the hot sun appears,
The racing river slows,
Villagers heave a sigh of relief.

Kirstie Bough (9)
Velmead Junior School, Fleet

The Sea

The sea is calm,
The sea is powerful,
The sea is like a pond,
The sea makes waves.

Under the sea is,
Animals like fish,
The sea horses float through,
The water as a fish.

Animals like fish,
Fly through the water.

Jannat Ijaz (7)
Velmead Junior School, Fleet

Amazing Things

Amazing things, full of colour,
Amazing things that make thoughts fly.
Amazing things make eyes dance,
Amazing things that make things swing!

Beautiful scenes, beautiful plants,
Beautiful humans, beautiful animals,
Beautiful mountains, beautiful hills,
Beautiful song, beautiful Earth.

A tiger's coat, striped orange and black
A glittery moon, shining silver and grey.
A very tall tree, stretching up to the sky,
A human body, as precious as ever.

But the things I like most are
A tiger's coat, the best of all.
Then a scene of a snow-topped mountain,
And last, the fascination of the human body.

Alexander Walton (10)
Velmead Junior School, Fleet

School Dinners

If you stay for school dinners
Better throw them aside
A lot of kids didn't
A lot of kids died.

The meat is made of iron
The veg is made of steel
And if you have the afters
You'd better make a will.

Claudia Rozier (8)
Velmead Junior School, Fleet

The Tenth Planet

What's that strange thing
Beyond Pluto?
It seems kind of small,
I wonder if there's strange creatures,
The come knocking on your door.

Although I think it's a great mass
It's as small as a balloon,
It might be a giant ball swept from the planet of Doom.
I wonder if it will pop soon, since it came from the doom.

It could be a meteor or a black hole,
But it could be a little star or another moon,
But I think it's the tenth planet although that it is bizarre.

Jorgia Flaherty (9)
Velmead Junior School, Fleet

Windmill

Windmill big and windmill strong,
Spin yours sails all day long,
While high in the tallest tower
Cogs and wheels grind wheat to flour,
The miller is a jolly fellow
By the name of Mr Mellow,
Come rain, come shine,
On and on works the windmill fine,
Sold everywhere in the village,
He's never had a little spillage,
At the top sails one plus three,
Day in day out go wheeeee!

Sophie Astles (10)
Velmead Junior School, Fleet

Monster Poem

Monster, monster under the stair,
He will strike when you're there.
He will snap! He will bite!
He will sleep away from light.
So beware . . .
He's right there.

Joshua Trafford (9)
Velmead Junior School, Fleet

The Fisherman's Tale

If stars were manta rays
they would slither across the sea
grey and flat,
the sea is dark blue and rough white
soaking everything in sight.

If stars were octopuses
they would suck along the seabed
green and slimy,
the sea is green and flat.

Zach Rowland (8)
Wallands CP School, Lewes

Mole

Worm muncher
brilliant digger
nocturnal mover
browny colour
good sense
blind eye-er
earth burrower
tiny traveller
soil scratcher
long liver.

Nathan Luetchford (7)
Wallands CP School, Lewes

The Animals Inside Me

There is a monkey inside me
Which is leaping from tree to tree wildly.
Diving down deep inside me
There is a dolphin.
Inside me showing his fantastic, multicoloured wings
There is a parrot.
There is a polar bear inside me
Who is resting from a cold day's fishing.
Searching for food through the rubbish
There is a fox inside me.
There is a robin inside me
Who welcomes people with his cheery song.

Lydia Powell (11)
Wallands CP School, Lewes

Inside Me

Inside me there is a whirlwind
that spins and spins and never stops.
Inside me there is a monkey squeaking
jumping from tree to tree.
Inside me there is a boy
looking at a Christmas tree in despair.
Inside me there is a hunter
leaving a blood track from a deer.
Inside me the world is opening
and all the joy is coming out.
Inside me there is a snake hibernating.
Inside me there is a flower
that's withering and dying.

Tim Herdal (8)
Wallands CP School, Lewes

The Cuteness Of A Mouse

Inside my head there is . . .
some fluffy cotton wool,
and a petal from a rose,
and a rainbow from a lost land,
and a snowflake in the sky.

Some pebbles and streams,
and a goldfish in a tank,
a shell and a stone,
some seaweed and a crab,

some pink eyes from a cat,
a stripe from a tiger,
a spring from a rabbit,
some fluff from a sheep,
the cuteness of a mouse.

Rosie Barker (8)
Wallands CP School, Lewes

The Animals Inside Me

Inside me, rolling along the jungle floor merrily is a hyena.
Inside me is a cheetah
Who runs along the African plains.
Creating a masterpiece with all the colours in the world
Inside me is a peacock.
There is wisdom flashing through the eyes of
The owl inside me.
Inside me is a wolf
Howling at the pure, full moon.
Free and flickering through the breeze
Inside me is a dove.

Laurel Emerson (11)
Wallands CP School, Lewes

All Covered In Mud

I heave on my green wellies with a mighty plop.
We set off on an adventure,
Not knowing what we've got!
We trudge along the garden path
Begging to go back.
The gate shuts with a thwack.
Now onto the bumpity track,
Trudging along behind Mum and Dad,
Wishing we could wave a white flag.
Suddenly godgy, wodgy, splat!
'Oh drat,' I say, 'now look at me!
All covered in mud.'
'Come on,' say Mum and Dad,
'We'll get you cleaned up at home.'
Turning back down the track,
Splat! In a puddle!
Opening the garden gate, into a muddy fortress,
Nudged by my sister and guess what,
All covered in *mud!*

Edward Powell (8)
Wallands CP School, Lewes

Golden Goose

Inside my head there is a sparkling lake,
a swan, a cygnet, a golden goose,
a rose, a rainbow and a pot of gold,

a castle, a shop, a pirate,
a patch, a seagull, a wooden leg,
a treasure chest, a parrot, a palm tree.

Juliet Blount (7)
Wallands CP School, Lewes

If Stars Were Angelfish

If stars were angelfish
they would dart across the lake of night
they would glimmer
like rainbows in the dark blue lake.

If stars were blue whales
they would plunge down into the depths
of the sea of night,
they would gleam
as they plunge into the water.

If stars were octopuses
they would wiggle their tentacles
as they floated around in the dark river,
with tentacles as green and slimy as seaweed.

If stars were dolphins
they would dive up and down
in the dark blue ocean,
shimmering as they dive
in the dark blue ocean.

William Wilson (7)
Wallands CP School, Lewes

The Animals Inside Me

There is a puppy inside me
Who is getting up to mischief.
Diving in and out the water
Inside me is a dolphin.
Inside me is a peacock
Swishing its tail in a lake.
There is a whale inside me humming a lullaby.
Shovelling its sawdust and food from side to side
Inside me is a hamster.
Inside me is a kitten
Purring and pouncing around.

Stacey Sedar (11)
Wallands CP School, Lewes

Water Would Not Have Warmth

If stars were sea horses
they would move through the water
as if floating through space
as if life didn't matter,
two hairs on a cat's tail
wouldn't be more interested.

If stars were sea horses
sea life would be exciting
never dart, just glide
through the shining sea.
Water would not have warmth
without these beautiful creatures,
oceans would not be kind
without these wonderful things.

Matilda Benjamin (8)
Wallands CP School, Lewes

The Dark Black Sea

If stars were blue whales
they'd plunge through the dark sea,
their beautiful blue colour
swimming in the blackness.

If stars were blue whales
they'd show themselves
beyond the darkness,
taking away the gloominess
of the black sea.

If stars were blue whales
the planets would dance around the sun.

Hannah Midgley (7)
Wallands CP School, Lewes

The World

Inside my head there's a dog,
a dog that bounces around,
a wolf, a coyote, a dingo,
a Dalmatian scratching at the door.

Inside my head there's a cat,
a kitten that has a secret,
a tiger, a puma, a cheetah,
a lion, a leopard and more.

Inside my head there's the North
and South Poles,
Mars, Jupiter, Venus,
a bear giving its paw.

Inside my head there's an Arctic fox,
a penguin, a seal, a polar bear,
an urban fox wanting food,
a rabbit, a whale, a macaw.

Inside my head there's a volcano
full to bursting with lava,
deep under the ocean it started,
now way up in the clouds.

Inside my head
is the fluffiest white cloud
way, way up
in the sky.

Inside my head
is the beginning
and the end
of the world.

Olivia Buckley-Jennings (9)
Wallands CP School, Lewes